SAINT PETERSBURG

history & architecture

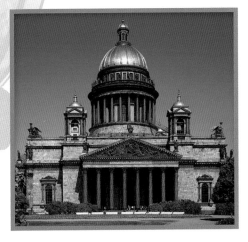

Яркий город

2010

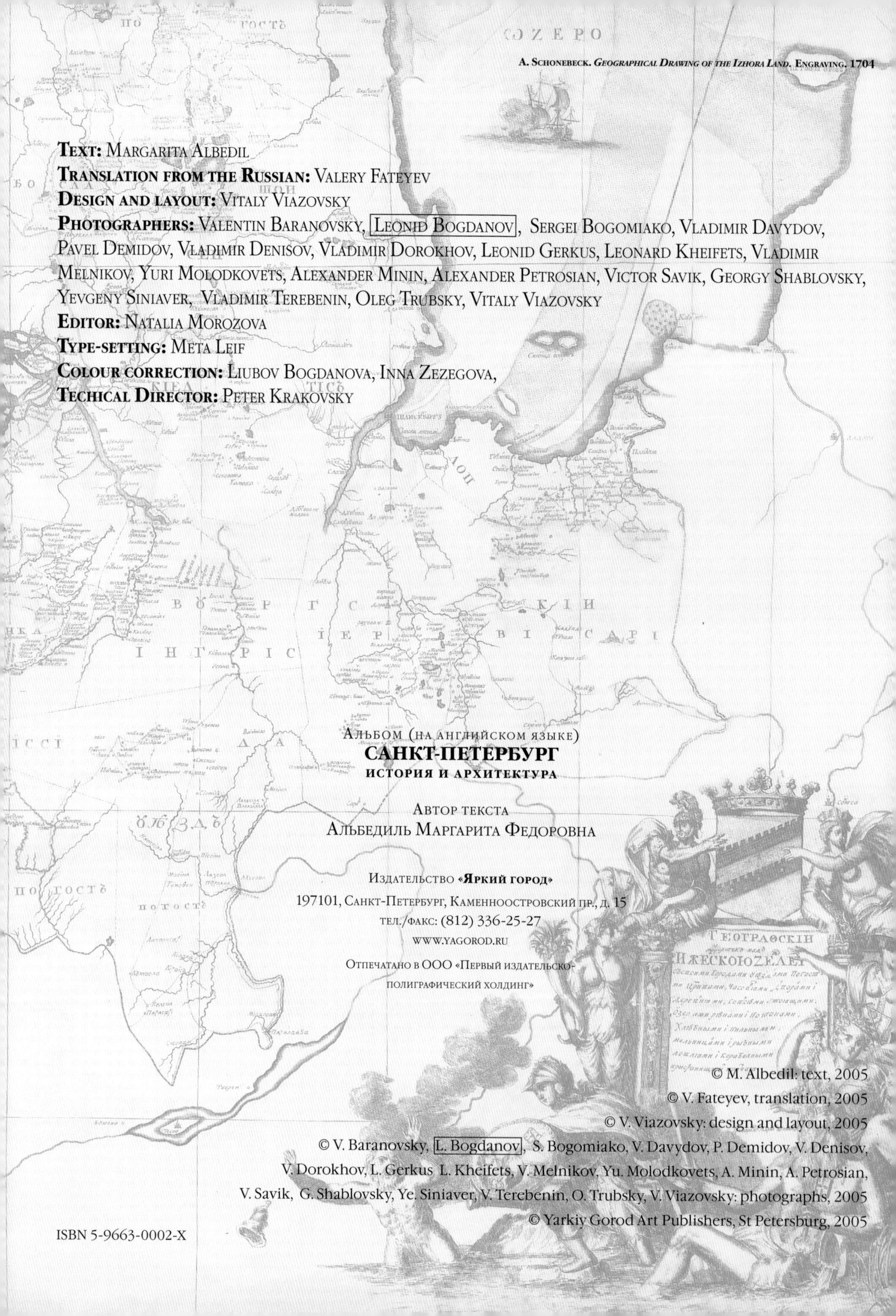

TEXT: MARGARITA ALBEDIL

TRANSLATION FROM THE RUSSIAN: VALERY FATEYEV

DESIGN AND LAYOUT: VITALY VIAZOVSKY

PHOTOGRAPHERS: VALENTIN BARANOVSKY, LEONID BOGDANOV, SERGEI BOGOMIAKO, VLADIMIR DAVYDOV, PAVEL DEMIDOV, VLADIMIR DENISOV, VLADIMIR DOROKHOV, LEONID GERKUS, LEONARD KHEIFETS, VLADIMIR MELNIKOV, YURI MOLODKOVETS, ALEXANDER MININ, ALEXANDER PETROSIAN, VICTOR SAVIK, GEORGY SHABLOVSKY, YEVGENY SINIAVER, VLADIMIR TEREBENIN, OLEG TRUBSKY, VITALY VIAZOVSKY

EDITOR: NATALIA MOROZOVA

TYPE-SETTING: META LEIF

COLOUR CORRECTION: LIUBOV BOGDANOVA, INNA ZEZEGOVA,

TECHICAL DIRECTOR: PETER KRAKOVSKY

Альбом (на английском языке)

САНКТ-ПЕТЕРБУРГ
ИСТОРИЯ И АРХИТЕКТУРА

Автор текста
Альбедиль Маргарита Федоровна

Издательство **«Яркий город»**

197101, Санкт-Петербург, Каменноостровский пр., д. 15

тел./факс: (812) 336-25-27

WWW.YAGOROD.RU

Отпечатано в ООО «Первый издательско-
полиграфический холдинг»

ISBN 5-9663-0002-X

The Sources

There are few cities in the world which have such a striking history as St Petersburg. Created thanks to the indomitable will of a single man, Peter the Great, the brilliant northern capital of Russia was destined to be born and grow on the swampy lands adjoining the Neva River. This north-east area had once belonged to the Vodskaya *piatina* or district of the Principality of Novgorod the Great. The banks of the Neva had since long attracted the Swedes who made numerous attempts to take hold of these lands. So it was important for Russia to strengthen the Novgorodian borders in order to prevent Swedish colonization. Great efforts were made for this purpose by the Novgorodian Prince St Alexander Nevsky (1221–1263). When the Swedes attacked the Novgorodian land in 1240, the nineteen-year-old prince headed the Russian army that defeated the enemy in the famous battle on the Neva River. In 1478 Muscovy annexed Novgorod the Great and the lands around the Neva became a part of the unified early Russian state, but only for a short period. After the Time of Trouble (late 16th and early 17th centuries), Russia, weakened by intestine feuds and outward enemies, lost its north-western lands. The Swedish troops occupied them and completely cut off Russia from the Gulf of Finland and the Baltic Sea. According to the Treaty of Stolbovo signed in 1617 the former Novgorod lands passed into the possession of Sweden and came to be known as Ingria (Ingermanland).

ICON: *ST ALEXANDER NEVSKY.* MOSAIC OF THE NORTHERN GROUP OF ICONS IN THE CATHEDRAL OF THE RESURRECTION
AFTER THE ORIGINAL BY MIKHAIL NESTEROV

S. PRISEKIN. *"THOSE WHO COME TO US WITH THE SWORD, SHALL PERISH BY THE SWORD"*. 1983
THE PAINTING ILLUSTRATES THE GREAT FEAT OF ST PRINCE ALEXANDER NEVSKY WHO DEFEATED THE SWEDES

St Petersburg: 18th Century

The Tsars had since long dreamed about getting access to the Baltic Sea and taking back the Russian lands seized by Sweden from Russia. With this aim in view, Peter began the Northern War in 1700 and led a successful attack on Ingria in 1702. To strengthen the captured position in the estuary of the Neva, he made a decision to construct a fortress on a small island called Enisaari, or Hare Island, by the Finns. The citadel was founded quickly and without pomp – the Tsar himself and his companions-in-arms could hardly think in those times about a new city and even less about turning it into the capital of Russia. The fortress-city of St Petersburg was growing fast, although gunfire could be heard roaring nearby. The crucial date for the burgeoning city was the year 1709 when the Russian army won a brilliant victory at Poltava. This victory changed the entire course of the Northern War and now Peter began to dream about a large city and a busy port like Amsterdam. He wanted to build on the banks of the Neva his "paradise", a symbol of new Russia. The beautiful new capital was rapidly growing on the banks of the regally powerful Neva.

JEAN MARC NATTIER. *PORTRAIT OF PETER THE GREAT.* 1717
THE TSAR-CRAFTSMAN PREFERRED COMMON WORKING
CLOTHES TO SUCH FORMAL GARMENTS

ALEXEI ZUBOV. *PANORAMIC VIEW OF ST PETERSBURG.* DETAIL. 1716
THE CITY RAPIDLY GROWING ON THE BANKS OF THE NEVA HAD LITTLE IN COMMON WITH RUSSIAN CITIES

St Petersburg is one of the first cities in the world built according to a previously conceived scheme. In 1716 the French architect Jean-Baptiste Le Blond (1679–1719), invited by Peter the Great, created a plan for the construction of St Petersburg and after his death in 1718 the work in accordance with this plan began under the supervision of the Swiss architect Domenico Trezzini and the control of the Tsar himself. Various specialists from Denmark, France, Italy, Germany and other countries worked in the capital of the future empire side by side with Russian craftsmen, so foreign influences were adapted to Russian town-building traditions. Dwelling houses, churches and piers were built by soldiers and war captives, local residents from nearby villages and convicts who were then sent to this large-scale construction site instead of Siberia. It took merely two decades to create on the banks of the Neva an unusual city that had no parallel either in Russia or in Western Europe. The newly built city, «of Northern lands the pride and beauty», as the poet Alexander Pushkin wrote, overshadowed old Moscow.

Within sixteen years after Peter the Great terrible fires devastated St Petersburg twice. Nobody undertook serious construction projects in that period – that was the era of coups and early dying rulers. It was only the light-hearted beauty Elizabeth, a daughter of Peter the Great, who decided, on coming to the throne in 1741, to implement her father's dream about the «northern Rome». In the twenty years of her reign St Petersburg changed its appearance beyond recognition. The efforts of talented architects, with the Italian Bartolomeo Francesco Rastrelli ranking first among them, turned St Petersburg into a splendid city of luxurious palaces designed in the whimsical Baroque style. This style perfectly accorded with the capricious character of the Empress and served as a beautiful setting for her resplendent life that was reminiscent of an eternal festival. Rastrelli's greatest creation was the Winter Palace, a magnificent royal residence on the bank of the Neva.

The architectural fashion, however, was changing meanwhile and Russia would not fail to keep up with a new up-to-date trend. A change in the style of construction became especially noticeable in St Petersburg during the reign of Catherine the Great, who ruled for 34 years from 1761 onwards. The modest Baroque predominant in Peter's era and the luxurious Elizabethan version were ousted by quiet and stately Neo-Classicism that reflected the worldview of the Age of Enlightenment. Its typical examples are the Tauride Palace built by the Russian architect Ivan Starov, the structures designed by the Scot Charles Cameron and the projects carried out by the Italian Giacomo Quarenghi. The «stately spirit of Peter the Great and the wit of Catherine», when combined, lent to the capital an imperial air of monumentality and resplendence. Europe was gazing in surprise at this Russian miracle: the northernmost capital that was growing on the Neva, as if by magic, amidst the woods, on swampy marshes. Foreigners coming from European cities with their medieval structures and narrow meandering streets, were struck by Catherine's St Petersburg with its wide and straight avenues, vast squares, elegant granite-clad embankments and magic White Nights. But what amazed them most was the sudden emergence of the city itself and its fabulously rapid growth.

CARLE VANLOO
PORTRAIT OF EMPRESS ELIZABETH PETROVNA. **1760**
THE EMPRESS WAS ONE OF THE MOST BEAUTIFUL WOMEN
OF HER TIME AND WAS VERY PROUD OF IT

STEFANO TORELLI
PORTRAIT OF EMPRESS CATHERINE THE GREAT. **1793**
CATHERINE THE GREAT THOUGHT HERSELF TO BE A FAITHFUL
FOLLOWER OF THE CAUSE INITIATED BY PETER THE GREAT

St Petersburg: 19th Century

Franz von Krüger. *Portrait of Emperor Nicholas I.* **1850s**
The reign of Nicholas I began with the suppression of military noblemen's revolt in December 1825

Adolphe Ladurner. *Ceremony of the Consecration of the Alexander Column on Palace Square in St Petersburg on 30 August 1834.* **1840**

In the nineteenth century St Petersburg spread along the banks of the Neva "as a marvellous monument to the victory gained by the man of genius over nature." Turned into the capital of Russia and being its main port now, it was quickly developing and getting rich. St Petersburg could boast a brilliant galaxy of talented architects in any period and never had a shortage of cheap manpower. Therefore nothing could prevent the Russian Emperors from endowing their northern capital with a befitting air of majesty and glitter. The first decades of the nineteenth century saw the emergence in St Petersburg of immense architectural ensembles on a scale that was unparalleled elsewhere in the world. The marvellous architectural complex of the Spit of Vasilyevsky Island was created, a major reconstruction of the Admiralty was undertaken and the Kazan Cathedral was put up on Nevsky Prospekt, the main thoroughfare of St Petersburg, enriching it with a new square. But the most impressive new landmark was the breathtaking ensemble of the three large squares – Palace, St Isaac's and Decembrists' (former Peter's and Senate) Squares. The focus of this ensemble became the new building of the Admiralty with its façade stretching for 415 metres. The tall golden spire soaring over its tower was crowned with a weathervane in the form of ship, a decorative feature that turned into a symbol of the whole city. Moreover, large-scale construction was under way not only within the city — a whole "necklace" of suburban palaces and summer residences was created around the capital by Peter the Great. Over the time they turned into brilliant imperial residences and now gladden present-day visitors as fascinating open-air museums. Many of these projects were carried out by Carlo Rossi, the favourite architect of Nicholas I.

YEGOR BOTMAN
FORMAL PORTRAIT OF ALEXANDER II. 1875
RUSSIAN MUSEUM, ST PETERSBURG
THE EMPEROR RECORDED HIS NAME IN THE ANNALS
OF RUSSIA AS THE "LIBERATOR" FOR FREEING
PEASANTS FROM SERFDOM

St Petersburg, the busy capital of a huge empire, a residence of the imperial court and military garrison, a city of officials and clerks, was thriving. But in the three decades of the austere reign of Nicholas I (1825–55), who was obsessed by a passion for order, the city acquired some resemblance to military barracks — it became, in the words of the poet Piotr Viazemsky, "slender, regular, aligned, symmetrical, single-coloured..." The inhabitants of the capital were afraid that under the new emperor, Alexander II, things would be going even worse, but the new rule turned out to be the time of "thaw". The main event of Alexander's reign, and probably of the whole history of Russia, became the Tsar's Manifesto of 19 February 1861 that declared the abolishment of serfdom. The reform changed the situation in the city: throngs of peasants rushed to the capital to earn their living. The new residents settled on the outskirts of the city where factories and plants were being hastily built. A large number of tenement houses were then constructed in the capital and they occupied whole quarters or even streets – they were put up closely one to another leaving inside them the "wells" of narrow courtyards.

Classicism with its harmonious clarity and balance, clear-cut rhythm and calculated proportions became out of date. It obviously clashed with the new spirit of practical pursuits that demanded comfort above all. The obsolete style was ousted by Romanticism with its spiritual and emotional thrust and a free choice of artistic means. That was the time of infatuation with the Antiquity and the Middle Ages, there emerged the Neo-Gothic movement, the ornamental trend, folklore architecture and other trends which drew in fact on all preceding styles. Illustrious examples of this period of eclecticism in architecture are the Nicholas Palace, the Palace of Grand Duke Vladimir Alexeyevich (now the House of Scientists), the Mariinsky Theatre and others. There emerged new types of buildings, such as railway stations, hotels, covered markets, banks, theatres and department stores. Drawbridges spanned the Neva, streets were paved with stone and provided with sideways; at the end of the nineteenth century electric lamps illuminated streets – in short, the city was improving its appearance.

ILYA REPIN. *THE MARRIAGE OF NICHOLAS II AND GRAND DUCHESS ALEXANDRA FEODOROVNA IN THE WINTER PALACE*. 1894
NICHOLAS AND ALEXANDRA WERE DEEPLY RELIGIOUS PEOPLE AND THEY PIOUSLY BELIEVED IN THE DIVINE CHARACTER OF TSARIST POWER

Emperor Alexander III, the "Pacifier", a mighty man of enviable health, died on 20 October 1894 from a kidney disease at the age of 49. The heir, Tsesarvich Nicholas, a man of average abilities, was not ready to take control of the huge country. Infantile, timid and shy at 26, when he had to inherit the throne, Nicholas was completely lost, and moreover, the political situation was rather difficult indeed when he succeeded the crown. On 14 November 1894 he urgently married Princess Alice of Hesse-Darmstadt, who took the name of Alexandra Fiodorovna after accepting the Orthodox faith. The luxurious and majestic wedding in the church of the Winter Palace was not accompanied by any especial merry-making and their honeymoon passed against the background of funeral visits. The reign of the last Russian Emperor began in a tragic atmosphere – during the coronation of Nicholas II many people were crushed by the jostling crowd. But except for the Khodynka tragedy, the course of life in Russia was still rather steady and quiet in the first years of his reign. Meanwhile serious changes were ripening. From the second half of the nineteenth century Russia was rapidly catching up with Europe — its industry had an accelerated development. At the turn of the centuries St Petersburg turned into an immense industrial centre. Changes in everyday life were unusually swift: many aristocrats replaced horse-drawn vehicles by cars; telephones, electricity, water supply lines and other modern conveniences were introduced. Modern trends in the design of clothes, hair-styles and a mode of conduct were changing as short-lived fancies. A new type of businessmen – bankers and entrepreneurs who owned large fortunes – have emerged. It was in this period that the last grand style, Art Nouveau, rapidly broke into the city's architectural silhouette. New buildings at the Petrograd Side and Vasilyevsky Island were so unusual in design that they seemed to implement the early Romanticists' dream of changing the world by means of beauty. Not only dwelling houses were then designed in the "Northern Art Nouveau" style – sometimes combined with Neo-Classicism – many banks and shops reminiscent of palaces by their richly decorated façades were also erected. The 1910s saw a rise, within this new stylistic movement, of a more experimental trend, Constructivism, that became especially widespread in industrial architecture.

A short period dominated by the Art Nouveau style– merely some three decades – was a crucial era in the history of St Petersburg and entire Russia. That was a contradictory time marked by an upsurge of creative activities of the Russian intelligentsia and a presentiment of an imminent catastrophe. The turn of the nineteenth and twentieth century coincided with a decline of old thinking and it was the northern capital that became the focus of intense spiritual quests and the main arena of the so-called Silver Age of Russian culture. The creative destinies of artists, actors, poets and musicians were interwoven no less whimsically than the lines of Art Nouveau itself. The atmosphere of the capital was permeated with mysticism and poetry. Disputes, lectures and editorial tea-drinking parties where writers and poets could meet with their readers were then popular; various ideas connected with the most profound and vital problems of the age were put forward. The uncrowned queen of this bohemian world was the poet Anna Akhmatova who held supreme authority in the Wandering Dog cabaret and became its symbol of a sort. The most notable phenomenon in the artistic life of the capital was the World of Art society, with the artist Alexander Benois as one of its founders. The World of Art members arranged exhibitions, issued a magazine of the same name and eventually formed a new artistic movement. They succeeded to show to their contemporaries the fleeting, phantasmal charm of St Petersburg, despite the then prevailing opinion about its exceedingly official character. Sergei Diaghilev played a special role in this circle. Energetic and enterprising, he organized the "Russian Seasons", a festival of Russian opera and ballet performances which enjoyed a great success in Paris from 1907 onwards. The turn of the century saw a growing passion for the theatre, although the inhabitants of St Petersburg had been inveterate theatre-goers since time immemorial. With the appearance of folk theatres all layers of population could acquaint themselves with this kind of art. Small theatres, cabarets with performing actors and private stages emerged in the capital. Worthy of special note among them was the theatre headed by the actress Vera Kommissarzhevskaya. It was she who invited the now famous Vsevolod Meyerhold from Moscow in 1906. Meyerhold, a creator of an avant-garde theatrical theory, believed that "secret doors to the Wonderland" were open to him as an artistic director, although many people regarded him as a mere "scenic juggler".

NATHAN ALTMAN. *PORTRAIT OF ANNA AKHMATOVA*. 1914
RUSSIAN MUSEUM

BORIS GRIGORYEV. *PORTRAIT OF THE STAGE
DIRECTOR VSEVOLOD MEYERHOLD*. 1916. RUSSIAN MUSEUM

ALEXANDER GERASIMOV. *LENIN AT THE ROSTRUM*. 1930

The age of Art Nouveau, seeking to innovate life and to tie it with art, suddenly had to face the terrible bloody revolution on 9 January 1905, when peaceful people were attacked by armed cavalrymen. The atrocities of the troops continued throughout the day, people were dying in the streets and it seemed that the capital was given for ravage to conquerors. The Tsar, scaring an attempt at his life, sat out at Tsarskoye Selo having relegated his duties to the subordinates. The circumstances resulted in an undeclared state of emergency.

This first Russian revolution, however, soon began to decline. Life in the brilliant St Petersburg went along the routine lines again, but not for a very long time. In less than a decade the events grew threatening again. In the summer of 1914 the capital of the Empire was shocked by the news that the First World War broke out. The city was soon seized with patriotic fervour and destruction attacks of all German companies began. In August 1914 St Petersburg was renamed Petrograd – the "German" name was replaced with a "Slavic" version. The giant state machine was collapsing; the Empire, like its capital, was in a turbulent state. In 1913 a luxurious celebration of the Tercentenary of the Romanov House was held, but four years later, in 1917, Nicholas II, the last Russian Emperor, unable to control the country any longer, signed his abdication. The Revolution of 1917 resulted in the fall of monarchy in Russia. In July 1918 Nicholas II and members of his family were shot by the Bolsheviks in the Urals. In February 1917 the state power went to the Provisional Government and later to the Bolsheviks headed by Lenin.

THE CRUISER *AURORA*. BUILT IN **1897–1903.** PUT AT THE PERMANENT BERTH NEAR THE PETROGRADSKAYA EMBANKMENT

TRIUMPHAL RETURN OF RUSSIAN SOLDIERS AFTER THE VICTORY
IN THE WAR OF 1941–45

FESTIVE PARADE IN HONOUR OF VICTORY DAY
WAR VETERANS ON NEVSKY PROSPEKT

An inspired orator with a keen insight into a mob's psychology, Lenin often spoke in public promising peace and prosperity at once after the elimination of the bourgeois power. It was he who became the head of the new government after the Bolsheviks had arrested the Provisional Government having its session in the Winter Palace. A signal for the attack of the former imperial residence was a blank shot from the cruiser *Aurora*. The radical Bolsheviks succeeded in quickly establishing their cruel regime in the capital. Troublesome rumours spread around the city; life was getting increasingly chaotic. In March 1918 the Bolsheviks shifted the capital of the newly formed state, the country of the Soviets, to Moscow. The loss of the status of the capital city greatly affected Petrograd – it lost its former glitter, money and power. Unemployment, devastation, famine, frosts and other disasters came down upon the city. Everything was frozen, from water supply lines to lavatories; people were dying on ice-bound pavements; they burnt furniture and books and demolished wooden houses for use as firewood. In January 1924, after Lenin's death, the city was renamed Leningrad and the authorities did their best to obliterate every trace of the brilliant past of St Petersburg from one's mind.

The twentieth century brought to the "granite city of glory and disasters" new unheard-of cataclysms, such as mass arrests and executions in the years of Stalin's "Great Terror", the War of 1941–45 (known in Russia as the Great Patriotic War) and the siege, unparalleled in the world's history. Hitler's armies formed a deathly ring around the city that did not come loose from September 1941 to January 1944. These "900 Days" mark the most tragic period throughout the city's history. Sometimes up to 30,000 people died of starvation in a single day. Not only all poultry and home animals were eaten up, but hungry people boiled leather belts, scraped glue off the wallpaper and ate peat. The former capital was on the verge of complete destruction, but it did not surrender. The people believed that once the enemy's feet had not stepped on its land before, it would not happen this time, too. The city withstood the trial, won a victory and repaired the ravage wrought by the war.

However, the stately and brilliant St Petersburg, as it had been in Pushkin's era, was gradually turning into a dull and featureless Soviet metropolis, Leningrad. "A window onto Europe" was closed, and now only rare ships from the West could be seen in the port. The residents of the once glorious northern capital began to call it bitterly "a great city with the destiny of a regional centre". One can hardly say now what would come out of it, where it not for Gorbachev's perestroika. Among the most positive changes it brought was a decision to give the city its historical name again: on 1 October 1991 it was officially declared St Petersburg.

St Petersburg: 21st Century

Monument to Peter the Great. 1768–82. Sculptor Etienne Maurice Falconet assisted by Marie Anne Collot

I n 2003 the revived city celebrated its 300th jubilee. In the past three centuries St Petersburg celebrated triumphs of imperial grandeur and witnessed terrible dramas of wars and revolutions. It was glorified and damned in literature – some authors saw it mystically attractive and some others found it disgustingly cruel. And even today it arouses different emotions, never leaving anybody indifferent. The inhabitants of St Petersburg believe that their city is the best in the world and capable to overcome any trials and tribulations. One cannot help musing upon the glorious and tragic history of the city near the equestrian statue of its creator, Peter the Great, the first Russian Emperor. This monument, a work by Etienne Maurice Falconet, inspired Alexander Pushkin for the creation of the poem *The Bronze Horseman*, and under its spell the bronze statue acquired a profound symbolic significance for St Petersburg implementing its spirit of vitality. Seemingly arrested in an eternal jump over the city, its patron is gazing, as it were, into breath-taking St Petersburg vistas and gorgeous ensembles.

An old legend has it that as long as the *Bronze Horseman* stands on its place, St Petersburg will not perish. Under its shelter the city's mystery and uniquely tragic history have blended to create that special unfathomable aura, which adds much to its everlasting beauty. The city has grown and developed as a living organism in the course of the three centuries and walking about it one can trace the principal phases of its life. The Peter and Paul Fortress will enable the city's guests to re-create the picture of its foundation; Vasilyevsky Island will probably help them imagine the time when there was a vast noisy forest all around; the Winter Palace and the Hermitage Museum will convey to them an idea of imperial majesty, while a tour of rivers and canals will add to their notion about the scope of work carried out on this swampy land to make Peter's dream about a flowering "Paradise" come true.

View of the Peter and Paul Fortress on a festive day ▶
The Peter and Paul Fortress, founded by Peter the Great, was a starting point of St Petersburg. The SS Peter and Paul Cathedral with its tall spire and many-tiered bell-tower, one of the city's main landmarks, is a symbol of the northern capital

The Peter and Paul Fortress

THE PETER AND PAUL FORTRESS. THE ST JOHN BRIDGE
THE FIRST BRIDGE OF ST PETERSBURG WAS BUILT ON PONTOONS ACROSS THE KRONWERK
PASSAGE IN 1703. SINCE 1887 IT HAS BEEN KNOWN AS THE ST JOHN BRIDGE

The fortress was founded on 16 May 1703 to the thunder of the enemy's cannon, on the low island of Enisaari ("Hare Island" in Finnish) near the right-hand bank of the Neva. It was designed to defend the lands of Ingria fought back from Sweden by the young Russian army in the course of the Northern War and to defend the mouth of the Neva. Fortification had a serious scientific background in those years and the plan of the citadel was designed by specialists. Tsar Peter the Great himself made suggestions on the overall scheme. At first they erected earthen ramparts with six bastions linked by curtain walls; a kronwerk protected the fortress from the mainland. On 29 June, the name-day of the Apostles Peter and Paul, and therefore of the Tsar himself, the city was given the name of St Petersburg. On 30 May 1706, Peter's 34th birthday, the Tsar founded the first bastion in stone – the future Tsar Bastion. This event marked the start of the reconstruction of the St Petersburg Fortress in stone under the supervision of the Swiss architect Domenico Trezzini. It was also he who began to build the stone Cathedral of SS Peter and Paul in 1712 on the site of a wooden church. Soon the entire fortress took the cathedral's name.

HARE ON THE ST JOHN BRIDGE. 2003
SCULPTOR: V. PETROVICHEV; ARCHITECT: S. PETCHENKO
LEGEND HAS IT THAT A HARE SAVING ITSELF FROM A FLOOD
ON AN ISLAND WAS THE FIRST CREATURE MET THERE

◀ VIEW OF THE PETER AND PAUL FORTRESS
AND HARE ISLAND

The Peter and Paul Fortress dominates the Neva by its powerful granite walls. Throughout the history of this fortified structure not a single shot was made from its bastions, although the garrison was always ready to repulse the enemy's attack. The fortress became one of the most severe prisons of Russia. Behind its walls languished Tsarevich Alexis, the son of Peter the Great, the Decembrists, members of the People's Will terrorist organization, the Bolsheviks and other prisoners. In the inner courtyard of the prison, besides the Cathedral of SS Peter and Paul, there is the Boathouse built to preserve the memorial boat of Peter the Great, the "grandfather of the Russian fleet". One can also see there the Commandant's House, the Mint, the Grand Ducal Burial Vault and other structures of various designation, now belonging to the "Peter and Paul Fortress" historical and cultural centre – a branch of the State Museum of the History of St Petersburg.

A RUSSIAN GUN OF THE 1813 MODEL ON THE LEFT FRONT OF THE TSAR BASTION

THE SCARP WALL OF THE FORTRESS WITH A SENTRY-BOX. 1703 ▶
ARCHITECT: DOMENICO TREZZINI. 1706–34. ARCHITECTS: DOMENICO TREZZINI, BURKHARD C. VON MÜNNICH. FACED WITH GRANITE IN 1779–85; RECONSTRUCTED IN THE 19TH CENTURY. THE CITADEL IS SURROUNDED WITH POWERFUL BASTIONS: THE TSAR, TRUBETSKOI, NARYSHKIN, MENSHIKOV, GOLOVKIN AND ZOTOV BASTIONS.

The Peter and Paul Fortress. The Peter Gate. 1714–18
Architect: Domenico Trezzini; sculptors:
Hans Conrad Ossner, Nicolas Pineau

The five gates of the Peter and Paul Fortress faced all the cardinal points. The main, Peter Gate is directed eastwards. It was built in the form of a triumphal arch and decorated with bas-reliefs. The central image, *The Magician Simon Cast Down by the Apostle Peter*, was interpreted in the eighteenth century as an allegory of Peter's victories in the Northern War over the Swedes. Under the bas-relief is fixed a lead two-headed eagle with a sceptre and orb weighing more than a ton. On either side of the arch, in niches, are statues of ancient deities *Bellona*, the goddess of war, and *Minerva*, the goddess of wisdom and crafts.

**The Peter and Paul Fortress.
Monument to Peter the Great. 1991.**
Sculptor: Mikhail Chemiakin

The Cathedral of SS Peter and Paul. 1712–33 ▶
Architect: Domenico Trezzini. 1896–1908.
Architects: David Grimm, Anthony Tomishko

THE CATHEDRAL OF SS PETER AND PAUL

MARBLE TOMBSTONE OVER THE BURIAL PLACE OF PETER THE GREAT. 1865
ARCHITECTS: AUGUSTE POIRAUX, ANDREI GUN.
FIXED ON THE WALL IS THE ST ANDREW FLAG IN MEMORY OF PETER
THE GREAT AS THE FOUNDER OF THE RUSSIAN FLEET

THE TSAR'S DAIS WHERE THE EMPERORS PRAYED STANDING OR KNEELING. THE CHERRY-RED LYONS VELVET OF ITS UPHOLSTERY BEARS AN EMBROIDERED REPRESENTATION OF THE DOUBLE-HEADED EAGLE, THE STATE EMBLEM OF TSARIST RUSSIA

THE CARVED WOODEN LECTERN WITH A CANOPY OVER IT. 1732
THE DESIGNER UNKNOWN; CARVED BY N. KRASKOP.
THE LECTERN IS ADORNED WITH THE GILDED FIGURES OF THE
EVANGELISTS AND APOSTLES, PAINTED INSETS AND ORNAMENTS

INTERIOR OF THE CATHEDRAL OF SS PETER ▶ AND PAUL. THE NAVE. ICONOSTASIS. 1722–26
ARCHITECT: IVAN ZARUDNY. THE UNIQUE CARVED
ICONOSTASIS IS DESIGNED AS AN IMMENSE TRIUMPHAL ARCH

EMPEROR NICHOLAS II AND EMPRESS ALEXANDRA FIODOROVNA WITH THEIR DAUGHTERS MARIA, TATYANA, OLGA, ANASTASIA AND TSESAREVICH ALEXIS. PHOTOGRAPH OF 1913

Nicholas II, the last Russian Emperor of the Romanov Dynasty that ruled Russia for more than three hundred years, was a tragic figure in twentieth-century Russian history. He abdicated on 2 March 1917 when St Petersburg and entire Russia got involved in the whirlwind of the revolution. Nicholas and his family were arrested and on 1 August were all exiled from their former residence at Tsarskoye Selo to the distant Siberian town of Tobolsk. Then they were transferred to Ekaterinburg and in the night of 17 July 1918 the former Emperor, his wife, their children and servants were shot in the mansion formerly owned by N. Ipatyev, Captain of the Engineering Troops. The entire royal family has been canonized by the Russian Orthodox Church.

TSESAREVICH ALEXIS. 1907. PHOTOGRAPH BY K. VON GAN

The SS Peter and Paul Cathedral occupies a special place among the churches of St Petersburg. It is the most important example of the Petrine Baroque and the tallest structure (after the TV tower) in the city: the height of its bell-tower with a spire and weather-vane is 122.5 metres. The many-tiered bell-tower with a weather-vane in the form of a flying gilded angel on its spire is an architectural landmark and one of principal symbols of the city that firmly established itself in the eighteenth century on the shores of the Baltic Sea. From 1731 to 1858 the SS Peter and Paul Cathedral was the city's main church and in 1858 it became the court cathedral. From the foundation of the city it served as a burial place for members of the Romanov Imperial House. It was here that the regal founder of St Petersburg, Peter the Great, who died in 1725, was interred. He was buried in the then unfinished building of the cathedral. A tradition to bury the members of the ruling dynasty in churches, widespread throughout the world, was followed in St Petersburg, too. A ceremony of carrying the body of the deceased Emperor to the Cathedral of SS Peter and Paul preceded the traditional funerary ritual. In 1998, the 80th anniversary of the murder of Emperor Nicholas and his family, their remains were buried in the SS Peter and Paul Cathedral, too.

THE CATHEDRAL OF SS PETER AND PAUL

THIS IS THE CATHERINE CHAPEL WHERE THE MEMBERS OF THE IMPERIAL FAMILY, AS WELL AS THEIR SERVANTS AND DOCTOR, SHOT IN EKATERINBURG, WERE BURIED ON 17 JULY 1998. THE TOMBSTONE IS MADE OF WHITE CARRARA MARBLE

The Log Cabin of Peter the Great with a garden and railing. 1703, 1844
Architect: Roman Kuzmin (stone protective structure)

The Cabin of Peter the Great on the Petrovskaya Embankment is the earliest wooden structure in the city that has happily survived to this day. Soldiers of the Semionovsky Regiment built it of carved logs in three days, from 24 to 26 May 1703, and on 28 May Peter the Great gave a house-warming party, in a solemn atmosphere, accompanied by gunfire, and settled in the wooden house having two low-ceilinged rooms. Undemanding in everyday life, Peter was proud of his unsophisticated peasant-type dwelling and called it "beautiful chambers". But he lived in the cottage only in summer and for a short time at that. After the end of the Northern War the Tsar began to erect formal residences for himself. Even in the lifetime of Peter the Great his first home was regarded as a historical memorial and in 1723 Domenico Trezzini constructed a gallery on pillars over the cabin to preserve it for generations to come. In the age of Catherine II the Cabin of Peter the Great was put under a new stone protective structure, and in 1844 the architect Roman Kuzmin redesigned the former pavilion and it is his version that has reached our days. In 1875 a small garden was laid out in front of the building and encircled with railings. In 1930 the Cabin of Peter the Great became a museum.

The Log Cabin of Peter the Great. The Dining Room

**View of the Trinity Chapel ▶
and the Mosque from the Trinity Bridge**
The Trinity Chapel is a symbolic memorial to the Church of the Holy Trinity, the earliest church of St Petersburg. It was built in 2003 for the celebration of the city's tercentenary

Vasilyevsky Island

Enjoying the panoramic view of Vasilyevsky Island that has preserved its unique architectural legacy of the three centuries, one can hardly imagine that elks abounded in this locality and so the island was called Elk Island ("Hirvisaari in Finnish") In the fifteenth century the Novgorod governor Vasily Selezen had his estate here. Having founded the citadel-city, Peter the Great placed an artillery battery under the command of Vasily Kormchin at the edge of the island and the Tsar used to begin his letters "To Vasily on the island." It is unknown today, to which of the two Vasilys the island owes its name. In the 1710s Peter the Great took a decision to make Vasilyevsky Island the centre of the developing capital and to arrange governmental establishments called *collegia* on it. The construction of the Twelve Collegia, the longest building in Russia (its corridor runs for about 500 m) began in 1722 to a project by Trezzini and lasted for twenty years, although the officials began to settle in it in the 1720s. The building became the focus in the layout of Vasilyevsky Island, the design of which was created by Trezzini together with Peter the Great, who dreamed of creating the Russian Amsterdam here. The austere geometric lines of avenues and streets on the island remind us about the Tsar's unrealized dream. The Bolshaya and Malaya Nevka Rivers, seemingly embracing the Spit of Vasilyevsky Island, are spanned by bridges connecting it with the left bank of the Neva and the Petrograd Side. The Bolshoi Prospekt leads to Pribaltiyskaya Hotel and the Sea Terminal.

MONUMENT TO VASILY. 2003.
SCULPTORS: G. LUKYANOV, S. SERGEYEV;
ARCHITECT: S. ODNOVALOV
THE LEGENDARY CAPTAIN VASILY KORMCHIN,
WHO GAVE HIS NAME TO THE ISLAND,
SEEMS TO HAVE A SEAT FOR A MINUTE
NEAR THE MORTAR BARREL.

PANORAMIC VIEW
◀ OF VASILYEVSKY ISLAND

The Stock Exchange

The grand ensemble of the Spit of Vasilyevsky Island, one of the most spectacular in St Petersburg, forms the central link in the panoramic view of the Neva embankments. The smooth river surface between Hare Island and the left-hand bank of the Neva looks like a majestic water square framed with fine ensembles of the city's central squares, but the Spit of Vasilyevsky Island had not always had its present-day appearance. In former times there was a port in this area and dozens of ships and boats were scurrying around on the Neva. In winter, merry-making and sledge races were arranged on the ice, and on Epiphany Day the Tsar reviewed the parade of the regiments at the "Jordan" hole cut through the ice. The Spit of Vasilyevsky Island took its present-day look by 1830. The floodplain was raised by filling it with earth and as a result the bank stretched out into the Neva for more than one hundred metres. Thus Stock Exchange Square was formed. Its main landmark was the Stock Exchange building resembling an ancient temple standing on a granite podium. The Stock Exchange, the Rostral Columns and the embankments of the Spit of Vasilyevsky Island formed the first large-scale Classical ensemble of St Petersburg. Nowadays the Stock Exchange building houses the Central Naval Museum.

THE SPIT OF VASILYEVSKY ISLAND. THE STOCK EXCHANGE. 1805–10
ARCHITECT: JEAN FRANÇOIS THOMAS DE THOMON
THE EAST FAÇADE OF THE BUILDING IS ADORNED WITH THE SCULPTURAL GROUPS
NEPTUNE WITH TWO RIVERS AND *NAVIGATION WITH MERCURY AND TWO RIVERS*

THE SPIT OF VASILYEVSKY ISLAND. VIEW FROM THE PALACE EMBANKMENT ▶
THE ENSEMBLE OF THE SPIT OF VASILYEVSKY ISLAND INCLUDES, BESIDES THE FORMER STOCK EXCHANGE, THE ROSTRAL COLUMNS, THE SQUARE AND THE GRANITE WALL WITH PARAPETS, DESCENTS TO THE NEVA, A SMALL GARDEN AND BUILDINGS ADJOINING THE ENSEMBLE FROM THE BOLSHAYA AND MALAYA NEVA

The Rostral Columns

VIEW OF THE SS PETER AND PAUL CATHEDRAL FROM THE SPIT OF VASILYEVSKY ISLAND. SCULPTOR: PHILIPPE THIBAULT
THE SCULPTURE STANDING AT THE FOOT OF ONE F THE ROSTRAL COLUMNS PERSONIFIES THE NEVA

There are two Rostral Columns on the square in front of the Stock Exchange. The 32-metre high red brick towers or lighthouses were used for their direct designation from 1727 until the middle of the nineteenth century, when a port was functioning at the Spit of Vasilyevsky Island. Inside the massive shafts of the rostral columns are winding staircases leading upstairs and there, on platforms, bowl-shaped lamps are fixed on metal tripods. Formerly they were filled with oil that could be burnt up, but in 1957 gas was supplied to the lamps that allowed to attain a fascinating lighting effect on festive days. The Doric columns-lighthouses are triumphal monuments dedicated to the naval victories of the Russian Empire. They are decorated with *rostra* – the prow decorations of ships (figures of sirens) in keeping with an ancient Roman tradition according to which victors in a naval battle brought with them the prows of captured ships, and the more of them the greater one's victory was regarded. The rostral columns are installed on powerful stepped bases, at the foot of which are set up huge monumental statues symbolizing the Volga, Dnieper, Neva and Volkhov Rivers.

◀ **THE SPIT OF VASILYEVSKY ISLAND. THE ROSTRAL COLUMNS. 1805–10**
ARCHITECT: JEAN-FRANÇOIS THOMAS DE THOMON; SCULPTORS: JOSEPH CAMBERLAIN, PHILIPPE THIBAULT, STONE CARVER SAMSON SUKHANOV

The Kunstkammer. The Custom-House

On return from his travel around Western Europe in 1698, where he saw Cabinets of Curios, Peter the Great took a decision to establish such a museum in Russia. He wanted to have a special building constructed for it, the house of learning and rarities or, as they said in those days, the "House of Solomon", after the wise Israel king. The Tsar wanted to demonstrate the entire science of the time in this universal museum, "so that people would see and learn." Russia's first museum was based on the collections of the Tsar himself. The exhibits included the famous anatomical collections of Frederick Ruysch, the zoological collection of Albert Seba and a variety of other objects strikingly unusual for that time. The building, unparalleled in St Petersburg for its design, suited the ideas of Peter the Great. Even today it stands out in the panorama of the Neva banks as a perfectly preserved example of the early Petrine Baroque. With the construction of the Kunstkammer the Tsar intended to make Vasilyevsky Island the centre of Russian science. After his death, fulfilling his will, as it were, the buildings of the Academy of Art and academic institutes and the Library of the Academy of Sciences were put up and the former building of the Twelve Collegia or ministries began to house the University. The dome of the Custom-House balanced the tower of the Kunstkammer and became an integral part of the ensemble of the Spit of Vasilyevsky Island. Today the building of the Custom-House is known as the Pushkin House – the Institute of Russian Literature.

THE UNIVERSITY EMBANKMENT. THE KUNSTKAMMER. 1718–34. ARCHITECT: SAVVA CHEVAKINSKY. 1754–58. ARCHITECTS: GEORG MATTARNOVI, NICHOLAUS HÄRBEL, GAETANO CHIAVERI, MIKHAIL ZEMTSOV

THE CUSTOM-HOUSE. 1829–32. ARCHITECT: GIOVANNI LUCHINI ▶

In 1709 Peter the Great presented Vasilyevsky Island to his favourite associate, the "Most Illustrious Prince" Alexander Menshikov, and soon a beautiful palace, the "Prince's Home", one of the earliest masonry building in St Petersburg, began to grace the area. Although nobody doubted Menshikov's low descent, he was lucky to become the Tsar's closest friend sharing the table, joys and troubles with him. The prince made a breathtaking career, accumulated unbelievable riches and was the first governor of St Petersburg. His palace glistened with luxury, especially striking in comparison with the Tsar's modest cottage. For a long time the Menshikov Palace remained the centre of social life in the capital, a place where official ceremonies and balls were held. Behind the palace there was a beautiful garden, the second best in St Petersburg after the Tsar's Summer Gardens, also decorated with Italian sculpture, and a stone greenhouse, the first in the city, were even tropical fruit ripened. The prince who had risen from rags to riches, walked around his garden shortly before his exile of 1727. He was deprived of all his titles, decorations and wealth in the reign of the young Emperor Peter II and died in Siberia forgotten by everybody. The building of the Menshikov Palace housed the First Cadet Corps in 1731. After the restoration of 1956–81 it became a branch of the Hermitage Museum devoted to the Russian Culture of the Age of Peter the Great.

THE UNIVERSITY EMBANKMENT. THE MENSHIKOV PALACE. 1710–21. ARCHITECTS: GIOVANNI MARIO FONTANA, JOHANN GOTTFRIED SCHÄDEL, ANDREAS SCHLÜTER, BARTOLOMEO CARLO RASTRELLI AND OTHERS (INTERIORS). 1730s–1740s. ARCHITECT: DOMENICO TREZZINI

THE WALNUT DRAWING ROOM, WHICH HAD THE SIGNIFICANCE OF ALEXANDER MENSHIKOV'S MAIN STUDY, IS ADORNED WITH WALNUT PANELLING ▶
PETER THE GREAT, EMPRESS CATHERINE I AND OTHER MEMBERS OF THE IMPERIAL FAMILY OFTEN VISITED THIS BUILDING

The Academy of Arts

THE UNIVERSITY EMBANKMENT. THE ACADEMY OF ARTS. 1764–88. ARCHITECTS: JEAN-BAPTISTE VALLIN DE LA MOTHE, ALEXANDER KOKORINOV

The building of the Academy of Arts on the Vasilyevsky Island Embankment, the construction of which began in 1765, was intended for the three main arts – painting, sculpture and architecture. Copies of the ancient statues of *Hercules* and *Flora* over the entrance and the shape of the building itself remind us of the two styles, Baroque and Classicism, predominant in St Petersburg architecture in that period. The project of the building was designed by Jean-Baptiste Vallin de La Mothe, invited from France in 1759, and the Russian architect Alexander Kokorinov (they are regarded as founders of Classicism in Russian architecture). A transition from one style to the other reflects the changes that took place in society. In keeping with the demands of the day, the Academy of Arts evolved a new system of the artistic perception of the world, when colour, light, composition and perspective were used to explore and render the unshakable laws of the universe. The model works by masters of the brush and chisel trained within the walls of the Academy, remained in it as model pieces to be followed. As a result a large museum of first-rate works of painting, sculpture, graphic art, as well as of architectural models and projects, was formed that ranks with the best art collections of Russia. Later many of these works were transferred to the Hermitage, the Russian Museum and the Tretyakov Gallery, but the Academy has retained the museum illustrating its history. Next to the Academy, at the granite embankment near a descent to the Neva, one can see the sphinxes brought from the ancient Thebes in Egypt.

◀ **THE UNIVERSITY EMBANKMENT.**
THE LANDING-STAGE WITH SPHINXES NEAR THE ACADEMY OF ARTS. 1832–34. ARCHITECT: KONSTANTIN THON

VIEW OF THE WINTER PALACE FROM PALACE BRIDGE. THE BUILDINGS OF THE PALACE COMPLEX ▶ ▶
CONNECTED BY PASSAGES HOUSE THE HERMITAGE, THE WORLD-FAMOUS MUSEUM OF ART

The State Hermitage

FIODOR ROKOTOV
***PORTRAIT OF EMPRESS CATHERINE THE GREAT*. LATE 18TH CENTURY**
A CLEVER AND AMBITIOUS EMPRESS, WHO RULED FOR 34 YEARS,
RANKS WITH THE MOST REMARKABLE MONARCHS OF RUSSIA

The Winter Palace, put up by Bartolomeo Francesco Rastrelli "for Russia's glory", the largest and most ornate building in St Petersburg, was the main residence of the imperial dynasty. It grew simultaneously with the city and within two centuries developed into an immense complex of palaces. A majestic example of the Russian Baroque, the Winter Palace, intended for Empress Elizabeth Petrovna, was completed in 1761. Elizabeth, however, died in December that year and it was Catherine the Great who became the actual first owner of the palace. In her reign the so-called *hermitage*, or a place of solitude – the then fashionable French amusement, as well as garden pavilions for entertainment and conversations "in the narrow circle of friends", were built. Paintings and precious objects, a prototype of the future museum, were also kept there. The Empress made the first acquisition in 1764 when she purchased the art collection of the German merchant Johann Gotzkowsky, who offered to pay his debt to the Russian state with the paintings he had amassed for Frederick the Great, as the latter failed to pay for them owing to the unsuccessful war against Russia. This year is thought to be the date of the establishment of the Hermitage Museum.

THE LARGE CARRIAGE USED FOR CORONATION CEREMONIES. FIRST QUARTER OF THE 18TH CENTURY. PARIS, FRANCE
THE CARRIAGE WAS BOUGHT BY PETER THE GREAT IN PARIS; PROBABLY IT WAS USED BY CATHERINE THE GREAT FOR HER CORONATION

◀ **THE WINTER PALACE. THE MAIN (AMBASSADORIAL OR JORDAN) STAIRCASE. 1754–62**
ARCHITECTS: BARTOLOMEO FRANCESCO RASTRELLI, VASILY STASOV

JACOPO AMICONI. *PETER THE GREAT AND THE GODDESS OF WISDOM MINERVA*
BETWEEN 1732 AND 1735. DETAIL. OIL ON CANVAS. 231 x 178 CM
THE ALLEGORICAL PAINTING GLORIFIES THE MILITARY
AND STATE GENIUS OF PETER THE GREAT

In 1941 a final decision was taken to reform the
Imperial Hermitage into a museum of world culture.
It was then that the Department of the History of
Russian Culture was created. It was based on the me-
morial objects from the "Study of Peter the Great"
attached to the Kunstkammer: after the Tsar's death
the materials connected with him and his time were
collected and preserved there. The Peter Hall or the
Small Throne Room, designed in the spirit of Late
Classicism, is distinguished by an especial majesty.
The Great Hall, the largest of its state rooms, occupies the central part of the Winter Palace.

THE WINTER PALACE. THE PETER HALL. 1838–39
ARCHITECTS: AUGUSTE DE MONTFERRAND, VASILY STASOV. THIS HALL WITH SUMPTUOUS DECOR WAS DESIGNED IN MEMORY OF THE FIRST RUSSIAN EMPEROR;
THE PATTERN OF THE LYONS VELVET LINING THE WALLS ECHOES THE STATE EMBLEMS OF RUSSIA AND MONOGRAMS OF PETER THE GREAT

◀ THE WINTER PALACE. THE LARGE THRONE ROOM (ST GEORGE HALL). 1838–41. ARCHITECT: VASILY STASOV
THE MAIN HALL OF THE WINTER PALACE CONTAINS THE THRONE PLACE AND THE CANOPIED THRONE; OVER IT IS A RELIEF REPRESENTATION OF THE VICTORIOUS
ST GEORGE, THE PATRON OF RUSSIAN WARRIORS AND THE IMPERIAL FAMILY

THE WINTER PALACE. THE MALACHITE DRAWING ROOM. 1838–39. ARCHITECT: ALEXANDER BRIULLOV
IT WAS FROM THIS DRAWING ROOM THAT THE "MOST AUGUST ENTRÉE" OF THE EMPEROR USED TO START BEFORE
THE OCTOBER REVOLUTION OF 1917. IN JULY 1917 THE PROVISIONAL GOVERNMENT HAD ITS SESSIONS IN THIS ROOM

In the west part of the Winter Palace, in the rooms of the former Large Emperor's and Grand Ducal Apartments, more than thirty rooms are allotted to exhibitions of the Department of the History of Russian Culture. Its very rich collections amount to around three thousand exhibits and cover a long period from the fifth to early twentieth century. These include ancient Russian icons, portrait paintings, historical documents, archaeological materials, weapons, banners and many other exhibits. The pride of the Hermitage is the unique collection of rare art objects in stone. One can see in different parts of the museum beautiful vases, chandeliers and table-tops of semiprecious stones brought from the Urals and Altai Mountains. The Malachite Drawing Room, designed by the architect Alexander Briullov, was the main hall in the apartments of the consort of Nicholas I, and from June 1917 the Provisional Government had its sessions there. Its elegant interior is trimmed with malachite; various table decorations of this mineral excavated in the Urals and produced by Russian craftsmen in the nineteenth century.

In the New Hermitage, walking around the magnificent rooms on the first floor, one can enjoy very rich collections of Western European art of the sixteenth to eighteenth century. The sumptuously adorned rooms and hall themselves strike us by their beauty and gorgeous details of their decor.

THE NEW HERMITAGE . THE RAPHAEL ROOM ▶
(HALL OF 16TH-CENTURY ITALIAN MAJOLICA). 1850S. ARCHITECT: LEO VON KLENZE

THE WINTER PALACE. THE BOUDOIR. 1853. ARCHITECT: HARALD BOSSE. THE APARTMENTS OF MARIA ALEXANDROVNA, CREATED BY ALEXANDER BRIULLOV IN 1841, WERE RENOVATED SEVERAL TIMES WITHIN FORTY YEARS IN KEEPING WITH A CAPRICIOUS FASHION. THUS, THE ARCHITECT HARALD BOSSE RENOVATED THE DESIGN OF BRIULLOV'S BOUDOIR IN THE ROCOCO STYLE.

The suite of rooms on the first floor of the south-east part of the Winter Palace was used in the second half of the nineteenth century as the private apartments of Maria Alexandrovna, the consort of Emperor Alexander II. They still retain their original artistic appearance to this day and give us a notion about living apartments of members of the royal family. On becoming the Empress, Maria Alexandrovna (the Princess of Hesse-Darmstadt before her wedding), lived in these rooms until her death in 1880 fulfilling numerous family and state duties. The Golden Drawing Room and the White Hall were official rooms whereas the other interios were employed for strictly regimented daily life. Today the Golden Room is used to display magnificent examples of Western European glyptics or carving of gems and semiprecious stones. Catherine the Great was infatuated with such pieces – she was an avid collector of cameos and carved gems and suffered, as she jokingly admitted, from a "stone disease". The basis of the Hermitage collection of glyptics was the collection of cameos bought by Catherine the Great in 1778 from the Duke of Orleans.

◀ THE WINTER PALACE. THE GOLDEN DRAWING ROOM. 1860
ARCHITECT: ALEXANDER BRIULLOV. THE ornate GOLDEN DRAWING ROOM
SERVED AS A FINE SETTING FOR COURT CEREMONIES

The Small Hermitage. The Pavilion Hall. The *Peacock* Clock. Second half of the 18th century. England. By James Cox.
The dial of the clock is concealed under the cap of the mushroom. When the mechanism is wound, music can be heard and bells are ringing. The peacock is turning and unfolding its tail, the cock is crowing, and the owl is blinking its eyes

◀ **The Small Hermitage. The Pavilion Hall. 1850–58.** Architect: Andrei Stackenschneider
The architect created this hall, reminiscent of oriental fairy-tales, on the first floor of the Northern Pavilion where Catherine the Great used to gather her "hermitage assemblies". The rich marble decor, crystal chandeliers and fountains by the walls fancifully combine the motifs of Arabian and renaissance architecture

THE OLD HERMITAGE. LEONARDO DA VINCI.
THE MADONNA AND CHILD (THE LITTA MADONNA). CA 1490–91
TEMPERA ON CANVAS. 42 X 33 CM. OF SOME TEN WORKS BY LEONARDO SURVIVING
TO THIS DAY RUSSIA POSSESSES TWO MADONNAS AND BOTH OF THEM ARE KEPT
IN THE HERMITAGE: *THE LITTA MADONNA* AND *THE MADONNA WITH A FLOWER*
(THE BENOIS MADONNA).

The Hermitage has been recorded in the Guinness Book as the largest picture gallery in the world. It is the earliest and most popular section of the museum. Its treasures reflect the main phases in the evolution of European art from the Late Middle Ages to the present day and contain works by nearly all leading masters of Western Europe. The celebrated picture gallery of the Hermitage opens with works by Italian masters of the Renaissance (late 13th to 16th century) displayed in the rooms of the Old and New Hermitage; one can also see there the displays of sculpture and decorative art. It is one of the largest collections of Italian Renaissance art beyond the borders of Italy. The pride of the collection are works by great Renaissance masters, such as Leonardo da Vinci, Raphael, Giorgione, Titian and Michelangelo.

THE OLD HERMITAGE. RAPHAEL (RAFAELLO SANTI).
THE CONESTABILE MADONNA. CA 1503
TEMPERA ON CANVAS. 17.5 X 18 CM. THIS PAINTING WAS
PRESENTED TO EMPRESS MARIA ALEXANDROVNA
BY HER HUSBAND, ALEXANDER II

THE OLD HERMITAGE. THE LEONARDO DA VINCI ROOM. 1805–07 ▶
ARCHITECT: GIACOMO QUARENGHI. 1858. ARCHITECT: ANDREI STACKENSCHNEIDER
THE ROOM WAS CREATED TO REPLACE THE ITALIAN HALL OF CATHERINE'S AGE

THE NEW HERMITAGE. PIETER PAUL RUBENS. *THE UNION OF EARTH AND WATER.* AFTER 1618
OIL ON CANVAS. 222.5 x 180.5 CM CREATING THIS ALLEGORY, THE ARTIST HINTED AT THE NECESSITY
TO RETURN THE ESTUARY OF THE SCHELDT RIVER, THEN OWNED BY HOLLAND, BACK TO FLANDERS

THE NEW HERMITAGE. REMBRANDT HARMENSZ VAN RIJN. *RETURN OF THE PRODIGAL SON.* CA 1668–69 ▶
OIL ON CANVAS. 262 x 205 CM. THE ARTIST CREATED THIS PAINTING BASED ON THE GOSPEL PARABLE AT THE END OF HIS LIFE
AS THE SUMMING-UP OF HIS THOUGHTS ABOUT ONE'S CAPACITY FOR LOVE AND FORGIVENESS — THE VALUES GRANTED TO US BY GOD

THE NEW HERMITAGE. THE LARGE ITALIAN SKYLIGHT ROOM. 1840s . ARCHITECT: LEO VON KLENZE.
INSTALLED IN THE CENTRE OF THE HALL ARE UNIQUE MALACHITE VASES AND TABLE-TOPS EXECUTED IN THE TECHNIQUE OF RUSSIAN MOSAICS

In December 1837 the Winter Palace was ravaged by a large-scale fire that lasted for more than thirty hours. Members of the staff managed to rescue the furniture and art objects, but nearly all the rooms of the palace burnt out. However, thanks to large-scale restoration efforts they were brought to their former brilliance merely in two years. This disaster led Emperor Nicholas I, the owner of the Hermitage in 1825–55, not only to renovate the old palaces, but to put up a new building specially for a museum, like those that had then appeared in Western European countries. The design of the building was entrusted to the Bavarian architect Leo von Klenze, who had built the Pinakothek in Munich. The construction of the museum entrusted to the Russian architects Vasily Stasov and Nikolai Yefimov was carried out between 1839 and 1852, and in 1852 the New Hermitage opened as the Public Museum. While formerly the Hermitage was considered as an integral part of the imperial palace and people had been admitted there only with special tickets given by the court office, now the collection became more accessible. The three main halls on the first floor of the museum, the so-called Large and Small Skylight Rooms, were intended for a display of large paintings – light penetrates into these interiors through the glazed ceilings. The Hermitage's collection of Italian art of the sixteenth to eighteenth century ranks with the best in Europe.

◀ GIUSEPPE MAZZUOLA. *THE DEATH OF ADONIS*. 1709. MARBLE. HEIGHT 193 CM. THE STATUE ILLUSTRATES AN ANCIENT MYTH ABOUT THE DEATH OF ADONIS, A LOVER OF VENUS, WHO PERSUADED THE YOUTH TO ABSTAIN FROM HUNTING AS SHE KNEW THAT THE JEALOUS MARS WAS GOING TO KILL HIM. ADONIS WAS TORN BY A FIERCE WILD BOAR AND THE GODS TURNED HIM INTO FLOWER CALLED ANEMONE

The New Hermitage with a façade in the Neo-Greek style and a portico with the powerful figures of Atlantes completed the ensemble of the Hermitage buildings running alongside the Palace Embankment of the Neva. It sometimes seems that the granite *Atlantes*, carved by the sculptor Alexander Terebenev and located in the niches of the ground floor to the left and right of the portico, support the leaden skies of St Petersburg. In 1861 the upper landing of the Main Staircase of the New Hermitage, the elegant composition of which is embellished with twelve columns of Serdobolye granite, was used to display the collection of Western European sculpture of the eighteenth and early nineteenth centuries acquired by Nicholas I for the Imperial Museum then under construction. The white marble staircase leads from the ground floor, from the rooms of new and ancient sculpture, to the Picture Gallery on the first floor.

The New Hermitage . The upper landing of the Main Staircase. 1840s. Architect: Leo von Klenze

The New Hermitage. Portico with Atlantes. 1848. Architect: Leo von Klenze; Sculptor: Alexander Terebenev ▶
This building was designed to house a museum, the first ever project of this kind in Russia, and even its façade resembles a museum display

THE WINTER PALACE FROM PALACE SQUARE. 1754–62
ARCHITECT: BARTOLOMEO FRANCESCO RASTRELLI. THE 200-METRE LENGTH
OF THE PALACE FAÇADE DETERMINES THE DIMENSIONS AND
APPEARANCE OF PALACE SQUARE

The building of the Winter Palace, one of the best crea-tions by Bartolomeo Francesco Rastrelli, is designed as a closed block with an inner courtyard. An architect of in-exhaustible imagination, Rastrelli designed all the fronts facing the Neva, the Admiralty and Palace Square in a dif-ferent manner endowing each of them with a uniquely charming appearance. The south façade became the main one – Rastrelli planned to lay out a vast square in front of it. This project was later completed by another great St Petersburg architect, Carlo Rossi, who created Palace Square. Facing the square were Her Majesty's Entrance that led to the apartments of the Empress and the Com-mandant's Entrance. On 25 October 1917 revolutionary sailors, soldiers and workers used Her Majesty's Entrance to break through into the palace and in memory of this event it has been renamed the October Entrance. On the day of the Tercentenary of St Petersburg, 27 May 2003, at two p.m., the Main Gate of the Winter Palace from Palace Square has been flung open and visitors to the Hermitage can use it again to enter the museum.

◀ **THE MAIN GATE OF THE WINTER PALACE FROM PALACE SQUARE**
THE RAILING OF THE MAIN GATE IS DECORATED WITH RUSSIA'S STATE EMBLEMS AND MONOGRAMS

Palace Square

PALACE SQUARE. THE ARCH OF THE MAIN HEADQUARTERS. 1820–28. ARCHITECT: CARLO ROSSI; SCULPTORS: VASILY DEMUTH-MALINOVSKY, STEPAN PIMENOV. CARLO ROSSI PUT UP THE BUILDING OF THE MAIN HEADQUARTERS AND THE MINISTRIES, THAT EMBRACED PALACE SQUARE IN AN ARC FROM THE SOUTH AND LINKED THEM BY A TRIUMPHAL ARCH IN HONOUR OF THE VICTORY OF THE RUSSIAN ARMS IN THE WAR OF 1812

◀ **PALACE SQUARE. THE ALEXANDER COLUMN. 1830–34.** ARCHITECT: AUGUSTE DE MONTFERRAND; SCULPTOR: BORIS ORLOWSKI. THE TALLEST TRIUMPHAL COLUMN IN THE WORLD, THE LARGEST GRANITE MONOLITH – A MONUMENT TO THE PATRIOTIC WAR OF 1812. ITS HEIGHT WITH THE PEDESTAL AND THE ANGEL IS 47.5 M. THE SCULPTOR GAVE TO THE ANGEL TRAMPLING THE SNAKE A FACIAL RESEMBLANCE WITH EMPEROR ALEXANDER I

VIEW OF THE WINTER PALACE, THE ADMIRALTY И ST ISAAC'S CATHEDRAL FROM THE NEVA

The three main squares of the city – Palace, St Isaac's and Decembrists' Squares – spread at the embankment of the Neva in the historical centre of St Petersburg, The concept of their creation was evolved by the Commission on Masonry Construction in St Petersburg established back in 1762 under the supervision of Andrei Kvasov. During the past centuries magnificent architectural complexes took shape here, in which perfectly blend masterpieces by Bartolomeo Francesco Rastrelli, Andreyan Zakharov. Carlo Rossi and other architects of different styles and ages, who succeeded to lend the city its "austere and slender appearance" eulogized by poets. The appearance of this part of the city reflects the lofty traditions of urban building formed in the eighteenth and early nineteenth centuries – the principles of "remarkable buildings", "regular squares" and "continuous linking of streets". The "water square" of the Neva separates by its soft lines the Peter and Paul Fortress from the regal Winter Palace and the resplendent Hermitage; St Isaac's Cathedral with its high golden dome echoes the tower of the Admiralty crowned with a slender spire, and all of these landmarks merge into a unparalleled architectural chord. The focal element of the complex of the three squares is the Admiralty, a symbol of Russia's naval glory and a masterpiece of world significance. The main thoroughfares of the city converge to its shining spire, the "Admiralty's needle", that seems to have pierced history indeed.

THE MAIN ADMIRALTY. 1730–38. ARCHITECT: IVAN KOROBOV. 1806–23. ARCHITECT: ANDREYAN ZAKHAROV; SCULPTORS: FEODOSY SHCHEDRIN, ▶ STEPAN PIMENOV, IVAN TEREBENEV AND OTHERS. THE BUILDING OF THE ADMIRALTY, THE TOPOGRAPHICAL FOCUS OF ST PETERSBURG, AFTER ITS RECONSTRUCTION BY ANDREYAN ZAKHAROV, BECAME AN ARCHITECTURAL HEART OF THE NORTHERN CAPITAL

THE ADMIRALTY EMBANKMENT. THE PALACE PIER. LION ON A GRANITE PEDESTAL. 1820–24. ENGINEER: ANDREI GOTMAN. 1900S (RECONSTRUCTION). THE FIGURES OF LIONS WITH LONG MANES PRODUCED OF SHEET COPPER AND SET UP AT GRANITE PEDESTALS DECORATE THE DESCENT TO THE NEVA ON THE ENGLISH EMBANKMENT — A RESTING PLACE OF THE CITY'S INHABITANTS AND GUESTS

THE ADMIRALTY EMBANKMENT. MONUMENT TO PETER THE GREAT ("THE TSAR AS A SHIPWRIGHT"). 1909–10
SCULPTOR: LEOPOLD BERNSTAMM. IN 1919 THE MONUMENT WAS REMOVED FOR ITS "POOR ARTISTIC QUALITY", BUT FOR THE TERCENTENARY OF THE RUSSIAN FLEET AND THE GREAT EMBASSY IN 1996 IT WAS INSTALLED ON ITS FORMER SITE

THE NEVA PAVILION OF THE ADMIRALTY. THERE ARE PAVILIONS COMPLETING THE WEST AND EAST WINGS OF THE ADMIRALTY ON THE BANK ▶
OF THE NEVA. COMPLETED AFTER THE WAR OF 1812, THE BUILDING WAS REGARDED AS A MONUMENT TO RUSSIAN MILITARY GLORY

DECEMBRISTS' SQUARE WITH THE MONUMENT TO PETER THE GREAT AND A GLIMPSE OF THE NEVA, THE ACADEMY OF SCIENCES, THE KUNSTKAMMER, THE ROSTRAL COLUMNS, THE PALACE BRIDGE AND THE PETER AND PAUL FORTRESS

A monument to Peter the Great was unveiled on 7 August 1782 in the presence of immense crowds of people. This event became the culmination of the jubilee celebration organized by Catherine the Great to mark the 20th anniversary of her reign. Seeking to take a legal and prominent place in the line of the Russian monarchs, she declared herself a true follower of the activities of the great Peter. The monument to the founder of the northern capital, to the "benefactor, reformer and legislator", was the first sculptural memorial in Russia. Catherine invited for its creation the French sculptor Etienne-Maurice Falconet; the head of the Tsar was modelled by his pupil Marie Anne Collot. The sculptor clad the Tsar not in the uniform, but in everyday garments and replaced a rich saddle for a beast hide. Only the laurel wreath and a sword at the belt indicate Peter's especial role as a triumphant soldier. The replacement of a usual pedestal for a large granite rock was also a bold innovation. Atop the rock resembling a falling wave, the "idol with a stretched out arm" shows, as it were, to the site where the new city is to be founded. The monument is regarded by inhabitants of the city as its genius loci closely connected with its spiritual essence. The *Bronze Horseman*, as the monument is generally called, became the focus of Senate Square encircled by the austere classical lines of the Senate and Synod buildings, as well as the immense St Isaac's Cathedral and the west side wing of the Admiralty. Renamed Decembrists' Square, it retains a sorrowful memory of the revolt of the nobles who mutinied on this square against autocracy and serfdom in December 1825.

MONUMENT TO PETER THE GREAT ("THE BRONZE HORSEMAN"). 1766–82 ▶
SCULPTORS: ETIENNE-MAURICE FALCONET, MARIE ANNE COLLOT, FIODOR GORDEYEV; ARCHITECT: YURI VELTEN

ST ISAAC'S SQUARE. THE IMMENSE BLOCK OF ST ISAAC'S SEPARATES ST ISAAC'S SQUARE, ▶ ▶
THE YOUNGEST IN THE ENSEMBLE, FROM SENATE SQUARE

PETRO PRIMO
CATHARINA SECUNDA
A... MDCCLXXXII

St Isaac's Cathedral

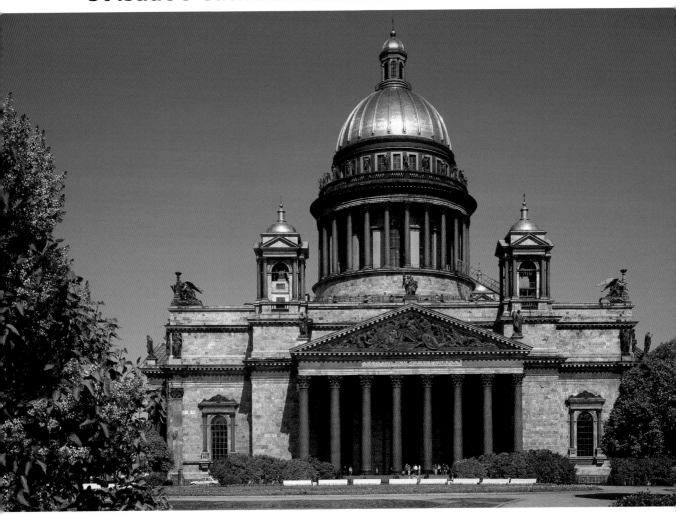

St Isaac's Cathedral (Cathedral of St Isaac of Dalmatia). 1818–58
Architect: Auguste de Montferrand; sculptors: Ivan Vitali, Peter Klodt, Nikolai Pimenov and others

S t Isaac's, like the SS Peter and Paul Cathedral, is associated with the heavenly patrons of Peter the Great. The Church of SS Peter and Paul, the earliest church in the newly built city, was founded on the Tsar's name-day and the second one was consecrated to St Isaac of Dalmatia, whose name-day coincides with the birthday of the first Russian Emperor – 30 May. Its foundations were laid on that day in 1707, 35 years after the Tsar's birth. It was in the first, wooden church that stood on the Admiralty Meadow that Peter the Great and Catherine were married. Later the church was reconstructed twice. The present-day cathedral, the fourth church on this site, was erected according to a project by Auguste de Montferrand, the "Architect to the Emperor" Alexander I. The impressive appearance of the five-domed cathedral towering to the height of 101.5 metres, suggested the steadfast quality of autocracy and the Orthodox Church in Russia. This majestic cathedral built for forty years, was a befitting completion to the age of Russian Neo-Classicism. It became, along with the bell-tower of the Cathedral of SS Peter and Paul and the Admiralty, a symbol of St Petersburg reflecting its inscrutable soul. Nowadays St Isaac's Cathedral functions both as a church and a museum.

◀ **St Isaac's Square. Monument to Nicholas I. 1856–59**
Architect: Auguste de Montferrand; sculptors: Peter Klodt, Robert Zaleman, Nikolai Ramazanov

ST ISAAC'S CATHEDRAL. DRUM OF THE MAIN DOME. CEILING PAINTING. ANGELS
PAINTER: KARL BRIULLOV, SCULPTORS: IVAN VITALI, ROBERT ZALEMAN, VASILY BELIAYEV

THE NAVE. THE MAIN ICONOSTASIS ▶
PAINTERS: TIMOLEON VON NEFF, FIODOR BRIULLOV, SEMION ZHIVAGO AND OTHERS; SCULPTOR: PETER KLODT. THE INNER DECOR OF THE CATHEDRAL STRIKES US BY ITS DAZZLING RICHNESS — MORE THAN FORTY DIFFERENT KINDS OF GEMS WERE USED FOR ITS EMBELLISHMENT. THE CATHEDRAL IS ALSO A VERITABLE TREASURY OF MOSAIC ART, FOR WHICH EARLY RUSSIA WAS FAMOUS, BUT FORGOTTEN IN LATER PERIODS. THIS ART WAS REVIVED BY THE FAMOUS SCHOLAR AND POET MIKHAIL LOMONOSOV. IT IS FOR THE FIRST TIME AFTER HIM THAT MOSAICS IN THE INTERIOR OF THE CATHEDRAL REACHED SUCH DIMENSIONS

**St Isaac's Cathedral.
Statues of Angels over the
colonnade of the central dome
and a view of the city from the
observation deck of the cathedral**
Auguste Ricard de Montferrand lavishly
used outside monumental sculpture for the
outside decoration of St Isaac's Cathedral
and created hardly not the largest
complex of this kind in mid-nineteenth-
century Europe. The statues of Angels
executed by Joseph German emphasize the
rhythmical articulation of the dome
and the slender shape of the drum

**View of St Isaac's Square from the
observation deck of the cathedral**
The ensemble of the square includes
the Astoria Hotel built by Fiodor Lidval
in the early twentieth century and
the Mariinsky Palace put up by Andrei
Stackenschneider in 1839–44 for grand
Duchess Maria Nikolayevna, the elder
daughter of Nicholas I. Today it houses
the Legislative Assembly of St Petersburg
▼

Nevsky Prospekt ▶▶
Photograph of the early 20th century

NEVSKY PROSPEKT. THE GOSTINNY DVOR SHOPPING ARCADE. 1757–85
ARCHITECTS: BARTOLOMEO FRANCESCO RASTRELLI, JEAN-BAPTISTE VALLIN DE LA MOTHE

NEVSKY PROSPEKT. VIEW OF THE ALEXANDRINE THEATRE. 1828–32. ARCHITECT: CARLO ROSSI
THE ALEXANDRINE THEATRE WITH A COLONNADE, SURMOUNTED BY APOLLO'S QUADRIGA, HAS AN ESPECIALLY FESTIVE LOOK BY NIGHT.

Nevsky Prospekt

NEVSKY PROSPEKT. VIEW OF THE BELOSELSKY-BELOZERSKY PALACE IN EVENING ILLUMINATION. 1800s
ARCHITECT: FIODOR DEMERTSOV. 1846–48. ARCHITECT: ANDREI STACKENSCHNEIDER

A large "perspective road", laid out in the reign of Peter the Great s the way leading to the burgeoning city, turned over the years into a brilliant centre of the northern capital decorated with magnificent palaces, elegant mansions and slender architectural ensembles. The name of the street stresses its link with the Neva: as a string of a huge bow, it connects the Admiralty and the St Alexander Nevsky Monastery located on the different sides of a bend in the river. Today this is the city's main thoroughfare, a street of museums and banks, churches and theatres, shops and dwelling houses. Its ever changing appearance reflects all the periods in the life of St Petersburg through the three centuries demonstrating a variety of architectural styles and a promenade along the city's main thoroughfare seems to be similar to a travel across the times. An incessant flood of cars, a lively public and attractive shop windows – such is the image of today's Nevsky Prospekt. In an evening electric light its buildings seem to dissolve in a vacillating and phantasmal realm.

The Kazan Cathedral (Cathedral of the Icon of *Our Lady of Kazan*). 1801–11
Architect: Andrei Voronikhin, sculptors: Ivan Martos, Ivan Prokofyev,
Fiodor Gordeyev, Stepan Pimenov and others

I n 1799, under Paul I, a competition was announced for the design of a new main cathedral in St Petersburg. It was to be consecrated to the icon of *Our Lady of Kazan* and modelled on St Peter's in Rome. The unknown architect Andrei Voronikhin, a former serf of Count Alexander Stroganov, President of the Academy of Arts, won the competition. The construction started in 1801, in the reign of the next Emperor of Russia, Alexander I, when the Empire style of Late Classicism was predominant. The cathedral was put up on the site of the former Church of the Nativity, where the especially revered miraculous icon of *Our Lady of Kazan* had been preserved since the foundation of the city. The architect made the main entrance to the cathedral on the side of Kazanskaya Street (the chancel should face the east and the entrance the west),

Tomb of Mikhail Kutuzov. 1813
In June 1813 the body of Field Marshal Mikhail Kutuzov was
brought to St Petersburg from Bunzlau. The Kazan Cathedral
was chosen as the burial palace of the Commander-in-Chief.
The decor of Kutuzov's grave was the last work
of Andrei Voronikhin in the cathedral

THE KAZAN CATHEDRAL

but decorated as the principal entrance the side one, at the north front overlooking Nevsky Prospekt. He erected there an impressive colonnade consisting of about a hundred 14-metre columns of porous Pudost stone. The gorgeous Kazan Cathedral was completed in 1811, before the Patriotic War of 1812 against Napoleon that aroused a general patriotic enthusiasm. The cathedral became a sort of monument to military glory: captured French banners, standards and keys of captured cities were kept in it. In the left-hand chapel the famous Russian army commander Mikhail Kutuzov was buried, and in front of the cathedral monuments to Kutuzov and another famous field marshal, Mikhail Barclay de Tolly, were unveiled in 1837. The heroic atmosphere of those years could be sensed in the inner decor of the cathedral looking like a majestic palatial hall. For a long time the cathedral housed the Museum of the History of Religion and Atheism, but in 1991 it has been returned to believers.

ICON OF *OUR LADY OF KAZAN*. 16TH CENTURY

THE KAZAN CATHEDRAL. THE NAVE AND THE CHANCEL. LITTLE HAS SURVIVED FROM THE FORMER ABUNDANT INTERIOR DECOR OF THE CATHEDRAL, ALTHOUGH 56 COLUMNS OF PINK GRANITE STILL SERVE AS AN IMPRESSIVE DECOR OF THE INTERIOR CREATING A FEELING OF GRANDEUR AND EXPANSE

THE SINGER & CO. BUILDING. 1902–04
ARCHITECT: PAVEL SUZOR; SCULPTORS: ARTEMY AUBERT, AMANDUS ADAMSON

The architectural image of Nevsky Prospekt produces an impression today that it was created, as it were, in one breath, following the concept of a great master. In real fact, however, the ensemble took shape gradually, starting from the age of Peter the Great, and became one of the most beautiful and comfortable streets in the world towards the middle of the nineteenth century. It was called the «soul of St Petersburg», «the focus of amusements, bustle and relaxation of the capital». «What does not glisten in this street, the beauty of our capital!» the writer Nikolai Gogol exclaimed. Towards the beginning of the twentieth century Nevsky Prospekt was steadily occupied by business people, owners of large fortunes, for whom huge buildings of banks, trade houses and company offices were built. They gave preference to the daring idiom of the new style – Art Nouveau. One of such buildings, put up for a famous American company specializing in the production of sewing machines, known for many years as the House of Books, can hardly be passed unnoticed. The imposing edifice of glass and metal immediately arrests one's attention thanks to its rising corner section crowned with a dome and a globe on a sewing needle supported by the sculptural group *Navigation.*

VIEW OF THE DOME OF THE SINGER & CO. BUILDING, THE GRIBOYEDOV (CATHERINE) CANAL AND THE CATHEDRAL OF THE RESURRECTION ▶

THE MANSION OF THE MUTUAL CREDIT SOCIETY. 1888–90. ARCHITECT: PAVEL SUZOR; SCULPTORS: DAVID JENSEN, ALEXANDER OPEKUSHIN

THE BANK BRIDGE. 1825–26. ARCHITECT: V. TRETTER, SCULPTOR PAVEL SOKOLOV ▶

The Griboyedov Canal

In the very centre of the city, not far from Kazan Square, Nevsky Prospekt crosses the Catherine (Griboyedov) Canal that was formed as a result of straightening the winding Krivusha River. Two strikingly poetic bridges have survived from the early nineteenth century in this area – the Lion Bridge and the Bank Bridge. Finished one after the other in the summer of 1826, they have an unusual design for that period: the cables holding the spans of the bridges are fixed on special supports concealed within griffins in one case and within lions in the other. The bridge with griffins, noticeable from Nevsky Prospekt, is known as the Bank Bridge, because it led to the gate of the Assignation Bank (now the University of Economics and Finance). Griffins were used for its decoration not by chance – they were regarded in the east as reliable guardians of hoards. St Petersburg architects, infatuated with exotic imagery from various ages, decorated the buildings of banks and joint-stock companies, in keeping with the fashion of the time, by such symbolic figures.

LANTERNS ON THE ITALIAN BRIDGE. 1950s
ARCHITECT: V. VASILKOVSKY, ENGINEER: A. GUTZEIT

CATHEDRAL OF THE RESURRECTION

CATHEDRAL OF THE RESURRECTION. *THE EUCHARIST*
DETAIL OF THE MOSAIC OF THE MAIN CHANCEL.
EXECUTED FROM THE ORIGINAL BY NIKOLAI KHARLAMOV

NIKOLAI LAVROV.
PORTRAIT OF EMPEROR ALEXANDER II. **1872**

The Singer and Co. building on Nevsky Prospekt affords a view of the many-domed and varicoloured Cathedral of the Resurrection standing on the Griboyedov Canal. The cathedral was created in the best traditions of Russian art of the fourteenth to seventeenth centuries and stands out among all St Petersburg churches by its distinct national appearance. This memorial church was constructed in 1883–1907 on the spot where on 1 March 1881 Ignaty Grinevitsky, a terrorist of the People's Will organization, mortally wounded Alexander III. So the cathedral owes its second, commonly used name, "Our Saviour-on-the-Spilled-Blood", to this sorrowful event. It is located at the very edge of the embankment where Emperor Alexander II was killed; in the interior this spot is marked by a majestic canopy of semiprecious stones. Outside, a special projection was made for the bell-tower that juts out into the river-bed at the spot where the Tsar was mortally wounded. Despite the sorrowful designation of the church, however, its richest decor lends it a light and festive appearance. The cathedral is lavishly embellished with decorative window surrounds and *kokoshniks* (arched gables), tiles and ornamental bands; its façades are trimmed with granite, marble and glazed bricks. The ornate domes are covered with enamelled sheets of copper and the dome over the chancel is coated with golden smalt. An important role in the decor of the memorial cathedral is given to mosaics on Gospel themes executed after sketches by the well-known artists Victor Vasnetsov, Mikhail Nesterov and Andrei Riabushkin. Their overall area is about 7,000 square metres. The cathedral is also remarkable for its richest variety of semiprecious stones, enamelwork and coloured tiles. The luxurious icon mount and the canopy are unique works of jewellery and stone-cutting. The cathedral was not a usual parish church and an access of common people into it was limited. It was used to read sermons and to carry out a commemorative service on the day of the Emperor's murder; separate services devoted to his memory were also held there. After the revolution of 1917 the cathedral became accessible to everybody and its decor was seriously damaged. In 1930 the cathedral ceased to function and was nearly destroyed. In 1956 the building acquired the status of an architectural monument and after a long period of restoration it became a branch of the "St Isaac's Cathedral" Museum.

CATHEDRAL OF THE RESURRECTION ▶
("OUR SAVIOUR-ON-THE-SPILLED-BLOOD"). 1883–1907
ARCHITECTS: ALFRED PARLAND, ARCHIMANDRITE IGNATY (MALYSHEV)

THE TENT-SHAPED PORCH OF THE CATHEDRAL
DEVIATING FROM THE ORTHODOX TRADITION, THE ENTRANCE DOORS
ARE SHIFTED TO THE NORTHERN AND SOUTH-WESTERN CORNERS OF THE
CATHEDRAL. THEY ARE DECORATED WITH FOUR PORCHES SURMOUNTED WITH
LANCET TENT-SHAPED TOPS

DOMES OF THE CATHEDRAL OF THE RESURRECTION ▶

CATHEDRAL OF THE RESURRECTION. *THE CRUCIFIXION*. 1907
EXECUTED FROM THE ORIGINAL BY ALFRED PARLAND.
THE MOSAIC ON THE WEST FAÇADE, *THE CRUCIFIXION WITH INTERCEDING
SAINTS*, INCLUDING A MARBLE AND GRANITE CROSS, IS INSTALLED OUTSIDE
UNDER THE BELL-TOWER ON THE SPOT WHERE ALEXANDER II WAS MORTALLY
WOUNDED. THIS MOSAIC WAS A PLACE OF BELIEVERS' ESPECIAL VENERATION
AND RELIGIOUS SERVICES, THEREFORE A WIDE BRIDGE THAT CONTINUED
THE SQUARE, AS IT WERE, WAS CONSTRUCTED ACROSS THE CANAL

CATHEDRAL OF THE RESURRECTION. THE NAVE. VIEW OF THE CANOPY

THE FOUR PORCHES OF THE CATHEDRAL, ITS FAÇADE AND INTERIORS ARE ADORNED WITH SPLENDID MOSAICS. MOREOVER, THE CATHEDRAL IS THE ONLY EXAMPLE OF MOSAIC ART OF THE NEW TIMES IN THE WORLD. THE OVERALL AREA OF THE MOSAICS IS 7000 SQUARE METRES. THEY WERE PRODUCED IN THE WORKSHOP OF THE FROLOV BROTHERS AFTER SKETCHES BY THE FAMOUS RUSSIAN ARTISTS VICTOR VASNETSOV, MIKHAIL NESTEROV AND ANDREI RIABUSHKIN

◀ **CATHEDRAL OF THE RESURRECTION. CEILING. MOSAIC:** *CHRIST THE PANTOCRATOR.* ARTIST: MIKHAIL KHARLAMOV

SALE OF SOUVENIRS AT KONIUSHENNAYA SQUARE. TOURISTS ARE OFFERED A WIDE VARIETY OF TRADITIONAL SOUVENIRS: FINE CHINA, ARTICLES OF BIRCH-BARK, CASKETS OF THE MOST FAMOUS SCHOOLS OF FOLK CRAFTS: MSTIORA, KHOLUI, PALEKH AND FEDOSKINO

Tourists are offered a wide choice of diverse souvenirs on Nevsky Prospekt and other streets of the city. Especially remarkable among them are merry *matrioshka* dolls that won world-wide recognition as the most typical Russian souvenir. Three to five gaily-coloured dolls put one into another take us back into the happy world of childhood. Russia had always been famous for its toys, but at the end of the nineteenth century, with the emergence of factory production, the toy-making handicrafts began to disappear. However, with the emergence of the "Russian style", at the turn of the nineteenth and twentieth century, traditional Russian toys attracted attention of many professional artists and they were studied, collected and recreated. A wave of interest in the national artistic tradition gave birth to the *matryoshka*, too, that became a symbol of the Russian style. It is based on the principle of the Japanese kakeshi doll, although somewhat similar toys were also made by the Slavs. At the International Exhibition in Paris in 1900 the Russian *matryoshka* won world-wide recognition. The first *matryoshka* doll was produced by the turner V. Zviozdochkin (1876–1956) and painted by the artist Sergei Maliutin (1859–1937).

The Roman Catholic Church of St Catherine

Peter the Great, building his northern capital, dreamed that all Christian confessions would have their churches in the city. His dream came true. When Alexandre Dumas visited St Petersburg, he called Nevsky Prospekt "a street of religious tolerance". The Orthodox Kazan Cathedral stands here next to a Dutch church, the Lutheran Church of St Peter, an Armenian church and the Catholic Church of St Catherine. The parish of the Catholic church was formed in the early eighteenth century and Peter the Great himself was the godfather of the first baptized baby. Three architects contributed to the creation of the church: in 1739 a temporary wooden church was put up after a design by Pietro Trezzini, in 1761 the construction of a new one in stone was started after a drawing by Jean-Baptiste Vallin de La Mothe. In 1779 Antonio Rinaldi, who was the syndic (representative) of the church, was put in charge of its building. The church was under construction for twenty years, from 1763 to 1783. It had many sacred objects and its decor was continuously improved.

PICTURE MARKET NEAR THE WALLS OF THE ROMAN CATHOLIC CHURCH OF ST CATHERINE

THE COMPLEX OF THE ROMAN CATHOLIC CHURCH OF ST CATHERINE. 1739–53. ARCHITECT: PIETRO TREZZINI. 1763–83.
ARCHITECT: JEAN-BAPTISTE VALLIN DE LA MOTHE. 1894. ARCHITECT: ANTONIO RINALDI (RAISING OF DWELLING HOUSES).
THIS CHURCH WAS THE MAIN CATHOLIC WORSHIP PLACE IN THE CAPITAL OF RUSSIA AND HAD MANY HOLY OBJECTS. MANY FAMOUS CATHOLICS PRAYED
IN IT DURING THEIR VISITS TO ST PETERSBURG – JOSEPH DE MAISTRE, ADAM MICKIEWICZ, FERENZ LIZST, ALEXANDRE DUMAS AND HONORÉ BALSAC.
THE INNER DECOR OF THE CHURCH STRUCK ONE BY ITS MAJESTY AND THE ELEVATED SOUNDS OF THE ORGAN PRODUCED BY GERMAN CRAFTSMEN
LEFT NOBODY INDIFFERENT. IN THE SOVIET YEARS THE CHURCH WAS USED AS A WAREHOUSE, BUT NOW IT HAS BEEN RETURNED TO BELIEVERS

THE MIKHAILOVSKY PALACE (RUSSIAN MUSEUM).
THE SOUTH FRONT. 1819–24. ARCHITECT: CARLO ROSSI;
SCULPTORS: VASILY DEMUTH-MALINOVSKY, STEPAN PIMENOV AND OTHERS.
1895–97. ARCHITECT: VASILY SVINYIN (RESTORATION)

The short Mikhailovskaya Street leads from Nevsky Prospekt to Arts Square (formerly Mikhailovskaya Square). It was traced in 1834 by the great architect Carlo Rossi, a master of High Classicism, who oriented one end of the street on the portico of the Perinnaya Line of the Gostinny Dvor Shopping Arcade and the other on the portico of the main entrance of the Mikhailovsky Palace that opens up immediately after the small garden in the centre of the square. Its majestic harmony will hardly leave indifferent even a subtle connoisseur of art. The main building of the Russian Museum, the Mikhailovsky Palace, Rossi's masterpiece, is recognized as a gem of world architecture. It was built in 1819–25 for Grand Duke Mikhail Pavlovich, the younger brother of Emperor Alexander I, on the place of old hotbeds and greenhouses of the Mikhailovsky Castle that became desolate after the death of its owner, Emperor Paul I. The superb palace was regarded as a temple of art even before it became a museum. The keynote of the architectural melody set by the palace is kept up by the other buildings on Arts Square, although they were erected by different architects.

THE RUSSIAN MUSEUM. ICON: *THE ARCHANGEL GABRIEL (ANGEL WITH THE GOLDEN HAIR).* 12TH CENTURY
FEW ICONS RIVALLING THIS PIECE IN BEAUTY
AND ANTIQUITY HAVE REACHED OUR DAYS

The State Russian Museum

ICON: *THE MIRACLE OF ST GEORGE SLAYING THE DRAGON.* **15TH CENTURY**
THE IMAGE OF THIS SAINT, A PATRON OF THE MOSCOW PRINCES, WAS USED FOR THE EMBLEM OF MOSCOW IN THE LATE EIGHTEENTH CENTURY

IVAN AIVAZOVSKY. *THE TENTH WAVE.* **1850.** THE ARTIST, WHO PRODUCED ABOUT SIX THOUSAND CANVASES, WAS PROUD OF THE TITLE OF PAINTER TO THE NAVAL HEADQUARTERS. *THE TENTH WAVE* IS HIS MOST FAMOUS WORK

KARL BRIULLOV. *THE LAST DAY OF POMPEII.* **1830–33**
IT IS THE BEST PAINTING OF THE ARTIST THAT HAD A TREMENDOUS SUCCESS ALL OVER EUROPE AND WON FAME FOR ITS CREATOR

ILYA REPIN. *THE ZAPOROZHYE COSSACKS WRITING A MOCKING LETTER TO THE TURKISH SULTAN.* 1891
THE ARTIST TURNED TO HISTORICAL SUBJECT MATTER SO AS TO BETTER UNDERSTAND THE SOURCES
OF THE NATIONAL CHARACTER AND REASONS FOR HISTORICAL CONFLICTS

The "Alexander III Imperial Museum of Russian Art" was opened in the Mikhailov-sky Palace in 1898. The building turned into a museum underwent serious alterations, which affected the inner decor of many rooms. Today only the Main Staircase, the Hall of White Columns and several surviving elements of decor remind us of the former magnificence. The collections of the Russian Museum constantly grow and today, in addition to the Mikhailovsky Palace, it owns the Benois Block, the Engineers' Castle, the Stroganov and Marble Palaces. The museum is justly called an "encyclopaedia of Russian art" – it preserves the most valuable artistic objects starting from the eleventh century. Works of all kinds of visual art, created both by recognized masters and unknown talents, are put on display. The museum boasts one of the best collections of painting by Russian artists, the largest assemblage of sculpture in the country as well as examples of folk and decorative and applied art. Displayed here are also rare ancient Russian icons, standing out among which are famous works by Andrei Rublev and Simon Ushakov. But the pride of the museum is a representative collection of easel painting of the eighteenth to twentieth century containing portraits, landscapes, genre scenes and other significant works by famous Russian artist of various trends. In terms of its scale and value the collection rivals the collection of the Tretyakov Gallery in Moscow.

Ostrovsky Square

THE ALEXANDRINE THEATRE. 1828–32
ARCHITECT: CARLO ROSSI; SCULPTORS: VASILY DEMUTH-MALINOVSKY, STEPAN PIMENOV AND OTHERS

Open towards Nevsky Prospekt is another architectural complex created by Carlo Rossi – Ostrovsky Square (formerly Alexandrine Square). Blending into a harmonious architectural melody here are the buildings of the Russian National (Public) Library, a small green garden with a monument to Catherine the Great, garden pavilions, lanterns and the Alexandrine Theatre (now the Pushkin Drama Theatre) standing somewhat apart. The theatre, a harmonious and ornate building, with the quadriga of Apollo, the patron of the arts, at the edge of the attic, is the focus of the ensemble. It seems that the building soars over the square blessing its builders. The theatre was named after Empress Alexandra Fiodorovna, the wife of Nicholas I. To please his wife, the Emperor ordered to make the furniture upholstery in the theatre blue like cornflowers – the Empress's favourite colour. The northern façade of the theatre overlooks Nevsky Prospekt and the south one completes the perspective of Teatralnaya Street created by Carlo Rossi and reminiscent of an ornate hall (it is known as Rossi Street from 1923). There is a small garden in front of the theatre where a monument to Catherine the Great was unveiled in 1873. The Empress is shown amidst her nine associates who contributed to her "golden age". In 1923 the square was renamed in honour of the playwright Alexander Ostrovsky.

◀ **MONUMENT TO CATHERINE THE GREAT. 1873**
ARTIST: MIKHAIL MIKESHIN; SCULPTORS: ALEXANDER OPEKUSHIN, MIKHAIL CHIZHOV; ARCHITECTS: DAVID GRIMM, VICTOR SCHRÖTER

The Yeliseyev Brothers Trade House

Simultaneously with the Alexandrine Theatre a new building of the Public Library was erected after a design by Carlo Rossi. It shaped the west border of the square, while its east border was formed by the pavilions of the nearby Anichkov Palace, also designed by Carlo Rossi. The earliest building of the Public Library had been put up back in 1796–1801 by the architect Yegor Sokolov at the corner of Nevsky Prospekt and Sadovaya Street crossing it. Rossi skilfully turned the butt-end front of the old library building into a side projection of the new edifice. He repeated the same device on the other side of the façade and added there a loggia with eighteen columns, between which he arranged windows alternating them with the images of ancient philosophers, scholars and poets. Their mute figures seem to watch passers-by hurrying to a theatre or library and at artists drawing anyone in a crowd desirous to have his or her portrait and at the monument to Catherine the Great soaring in the centre of a little garden.

INTERIOR OF THE YELISEYEV BROTHERS TRADE HOUSE

On Nevsky Prospekt, opposite the small Catherine Garden, there stands a gorgeous building – the trade house of the Yeliseyev merchant family. Built at the beginning of the twentieth century in stone, concrete and glass, it has many strikingly impressive details: a huge glazed surface of the façade, a large stained glass window, heavy stone facing, ponderous, naturalistic sculpture and fanciful curvilinear ornaments typical of the Art Nouveau style. The arch or stained-glass window is embellished with the allegorical figures of Industry, *Trade, Art* and *Science*. A combination in one building of diverse establishments is another unusual feature – there is a shop on the ground floor, a theatre as well as a casino and a bank on the first floor. The rich decor of the trade halls also produces an indelible impression: exotic and diversely decorated showcases are illuminated by fanciful wall lamps. Like in the days of its owners, the building houses one of the best grocer's shops of St Petersburg, with a plentiful supply of local and exotic goods. In the depth of the Yeliseyev shop porch there is an entrance to the Comedy Theatre that was headed for a long time by Nikolai Akimov, who was dubbed "the Mozart of humour".

THE BROTHERS YELISEYEV TRADE HOUSE. STATUE *ART* ON THE FRONT OF THE BUILDING

MALAYA SADOVAYA STREET

MALAYA SADOVAYA STREET. MONUMENT TO THE ST PETERSBURG PHOTOGRAPHER. 2001
SCULPTOR: B. PETROV. IN THE EIGHTEENTH CENTURY THE TRACT OF LAND BETWEEN NEVSKY PROSPEKT, SADOVAYA, ITALIANSKAYA AND MALAYA SADOVAYA STREETS WAS OCCUPIED BY THE ESTATE OF COUNT IVAN SHUVALOV WITH AN IMMENSE PALACE, A VAST GARDEN AND A LARGE COURTYARD. HE SOLD IT BY THE EARLY NINETEENTH CENTURY WHEN THE LAND GREW MORE EXPENSIVE. TOWARDS THE END OF THE CENTURY A LARGE NUMBER OF TENEMENT HOUSES APPEARED ON THIS SITE. THE GROUND FLOORS OF THESE HOUSES WERE USUALLY TAKEN BY BANKS, SHOPS WITH HUGE SHOWCASES OR CAFÉS. THE ATMOSPHERE OF THIS PERIOD IS WELL ILLUSTRATED BY OLD PHOTOGRAPHS FAITHFULLY FEATURING THE CITY'S LIFE

Malaya Sadovaya Street

THE "GOOD DOG" COURTYARD. IN A COURTYARD ON MALAYA SADOVAYA STREET THERE IS A MONUMENT TO GAVRIUSHA, A STRAY DOG, EXECUTED BY THE SCULPTOR V. SIVAKOV IN 1999. RESIDENTS OF THE CITY AND ITS GUESTS COME TO THIS COURTYARD IN A HOPE THAT THEIR MOST CHERISHED WISHES WILL COME TRUE — ONE CAN DROP A LETTER WITH ONE'S WISHES INTO A «MAILBOX OF DREAM» OR CAN WRITE THEM DIRECTLY ON THE WALL

Not a single generation of St Petersburg architects was engaged in the improvement and decoration of Nevsky Prospekt. Present-day architects continue these glorious historical traditions combining the established canons with new architectural demands, skilfully playing on the restrained St Petersburg palette. In recent years pedestrian zones were created on Malaya Koniushennaya and Malaya Sadovaya Streets running from Nevsky Prospekt and new monuments and "small forms" were installed there: *Ostap Bender*, an adventurer from literary bestsellers, *The Policeman* and *The Photographer* – a generalized image reminiscent of the famous Karl Bulla. One can unhurriedly walk along these pedestrian streets, drop into a café or a shop. There are many memorable places in this area. For instance, at the beginning of the twentieth century there was the Noble Assembly at the corner of Malaya Sadovaya and Italianskaya Street. After the revolution it ceased to exist and the then famous Proletkult ("Proletarian Culture") art organization occupied the building. Today it is the House of Radio and all elderly inhabitants of the city recall the voices that sounded from it during the harsh years of the siege.

FOUNTAIN ON MALAYA SADOVAYA STREET

The Beloselsky–Belozersky Palace

THE BELOSELSKY-BELOZERSKY PALACE. 1846–48. ARCHITECT: ANDREI STACKENSCHNEIDER

At the crossing of Nevsky Prospekt and the Fontanka River there was the city's boundary in the first quarter of the eighteenth century. So a bridge was built across the river by soldiers of the regiment that quartered nearby and was headed by Lieutenant Colonel Anichkov. The bridge, functioning without a major reconstruction for three centuries, has retained its original name. It has acquired its present-day appearance in the first half of the nineteenth century, when it was decorated with four sculptural figures of horse tamers personifying various phases of man's struggle with a horse for taming it to complete subordination. The sculptural groups were produced by the eminent St Petersburg sculptor Peter Klodt and therefore the city's inhabitants sometimes call them «Klodt's horses». Behind the bridge there stands an attractive mansion that before the Revolution of 1917 belonged to Princes Beloselsky-Belozersky, who traced their family line to Vladimir Monomakh and Yuri Dolgoruky. Reconstructing an old house that stood on this site, the architect Andrei Stackenschneider created a mansion in the so-called «Second Baroque» style, inspired by the Baroque features of the similarly disposed Stroganov Palace at the corner of Nevsky Prospekt and the Moika River. Today the Beloselsky-Belozersky Palace houses the municipal cultural centre of St Petersburg.

◀ THE ANICHKOV BRIDGE. 1839–41. ENGINEERS: ANDREI GOTMAN, I. BUTATS.
SCULPTURAL GROUP: *TAMING A HORSE*. 1839–50. SCULPTOR PETER KLODT

The Fontanka River is a branch of the Neva that crosses the main streets of the city and empties its waters into the main river again near its estuary. Its earliest name is unknown, but at the beginning of the eighteenth century it was called the Nameless Channel. The present-day name of the river is connected with the fact that it supplied water for fountains that had functioned in the Summer Gardens in Peter's age. There are many beautiful bridges spanning the Fontanka and many other rivers and canals, a feature that adds much to the city's romantic appearance – it is not for nothing that the northern capital is sometimes called the city of bridges or even a museum of bridges. Indeed, there are more of them here than in any other city in the world, except, perhaps, for Venice, although Peter the Great, the founder of St Petersburg, did not encourage the construction of bridges. He believed that the residents of the city should move along the Neva and its tributaries, in boats in summer and over the ice in winter. Permanent stone bridges across the Fontanka appeared only in the 1780s. All of them had three spans and their piers were designed as granite towers. But such towers with chains in the spirit of the age of Catherine the Great have survived only on two bridges – the Old Kalinkin Bridge and the Lomonosov (formerly Chernyshev) Bridge.

THE LOMONOSOV (CHERNYSHEV) BRIDGE. 1785–87. IN THE 1780S SEVEN SIMILAR BRIDGES OF THIS TYPE WERE BUILT ACROSS THE FONTANKA RIVER. EACH OF THEM HAD FOUR GRANITE PAVILIONS CONCEALING LIFTING MECHANISMS THAT PULLED THE CHAINS AND OPENED UP THE WINGS OF THE MIDDLE SPAN. TWO OF THEM, THE LOMONOSOV (FORMERLY CHERNYSHEV) AND THE OLD KALINKIN BRIDGES, HAVE SURVIVED

THE EGYPTIAN BRIDGE ACROSS THE FONTANKA. 1825–26 ▶
ENGINEERS: G. TRETTER, V. KHRISTIANOVICH. 1954–56. ENGINEER: V. DEMCHENKO; ARCHITECT: P. ARESHEV
ORIGINALLY THE BRIDGE HAD A SUSPENSION DESIGN AND SERVED TO THE CITY FOR 79 YEARS, BUT IN 1905 IT COLLAPSED
UNDER THE WEIGHT OF THE SQUADRON OF CAVALRY GUARDS. AT THE ENTRY TO THE NEW BRIDGE BUILT IN THE MIDDLE
OF THE TWENTIETH CENTURY, THERE ARE, AS BEFORE, CAST-IRON SPHINXES TOWERING ON GRANITE PEDESTALS

The St Alexander Nevsky Monastery

In 1710 Peter the Great chose a spot where the Black River (now the Monastyrka) flows into the Neva and ordered to build a monastery there "in the name of the Holy Trinity and the Saint Grand Prince Alexander Nevsky". Tradition has it that on this site the grand prince won a victory over the Swedes in 1240. People's memory about this event turned out to be important politically – the young capital needed one more spiritual patron in addition to St Peter and St Alexander Nevsky was a suitable figure for that purpose. So Peter the Great made up his mind to construct a sort of memorial monastery in this place. Its construction lasted throughout the eighteenth century in keeping with the original project by Domenico Trezzini – to create not just a monastery, but at the same time the residence of the Metropolitans, an official establishment and a palace. In the 1720s the holy relics of St Alexander Nevsky were brought to the monastery and eventually it received the title of *laura*, one of the most important monasteries. The Alexander-Nevsky Monastery (Laura) serves as a harmonious completion to Nevsky Prospekt. Today its complex includes more than ten churches, cells, diverse monastery structures and several cemeteries. From the time of its foundation the monastery served as the most significant burial place of imperial Russia, so many members of the imperial dynasty, outstanding men of letters and arts, prominent soldiers and statesmen were buried there.

THE ST ALEXANDER NEVSKY MONASTERY OF THE HOLY TRINITY. CATHEDRAL OF THE HOLY TRINITY. 1776–90
ARCHITECT: IVAN STAROV; SCULPTOR FEDOT SHUBIN

THE ST ALEXANDER NEVSKY MONASTERY OF THE HOLY TRINITY. VIEW OF THE ANNUNCIATION CHURCH. 1717–23

NECROPOLIS OF THE MASTERS OF ART.
TOMBSTONE OF FIODOR DOSTOYEVSKY. 1883
ARCHITECT: CHRISANPH VASILYEV; SCULPTOR NIKOLAI LAVERETSKY

NECROPOLIS OF THE MASTERS OF ART.
TOMBSTONE OF PIOTR TCHAIKOVSKY. 1897
SCULPTOR PAVEL KAMENSKY

The Smolny Convent

THE SMOLNY CATHEDRAL (CATHEDRAL OF THE RESURRECTION OF THE SMOLNY CONVENT). 1748–62
ARCHITECT: BARTOLOMEO FRANCESCO RASTRELLI. 1762–69. ARCHITECT: YURI VELTEN. 1832–35. ARCHITECT: VASILY STASOV

The pious Empress Elizabeth thought from time to time about retiring to a convent. The first stone convent in St Petersburg, well seen from the Neva, was opened at her behest. The site for it was chosen near the Tar Yard of Peter the Great where Elizabeth, then a Tsesarevna, had lived in a wooden house, and hence the name of the cloister – the Smolny Convent (*smola* means "tar" in Russian). The cathedral of the convent, founded in 1748, was built by Bartolomeo Francesco Rastrelli and the majestic, edifice soaring upwards became one of the most perfect creations both of the great architect and the entire Russian Baroque. The cathedral, cross-shaped in plan, consists of the nunnery, refectory, library, the apartments of the mother superior and four corner churches. Rastrelli wanted to put up a gigantic bell-tower 140 metres high over the entrance to the convent, but first the Seven-Year War and then the death of Elizabeth prevented him from fulfilling his dream. Years passed and it seemed that everybody forgot about the cathedral. It was only in 1828 that Vasily Stasov completed the work. In 1835 the cathedral was consecrated, but there was never any convent within its wall. In 1923 the cathedral was closed and for a long time served as a warehouse. Now, after restoration, the building houses a museum.

◀ DOMES OF THE SMOLNY CATHEDRAL

The Summer Gardens. *Nymph. Navigation.* **Early 18th century**
Anonymous sculptor

The Summer Gardens. *Nymph (Flora).* **Late 18th century**
Sculptor: Thomas Quellinus

The Summer Gardens. Bust: *Clarity.* **Early 18th century**
Anonymous sculptor

T he Summer Gardens, the earliest in St Petersburg, are of the same age as the city: they were laid out in 1704, soon after the foundation of St Petersburg. The Russian architect I. Ugriumov was put in charge of the garden's layout and the Tsar himself supervised the work giving orders to bring plants, bushes and trees from all corners of Russia. Peter's favourite gardens face the Neva with its northern, main part and the southern one overlooks the Moika, while the east border passes along the Fontanka embankment and the west one is marked by the Swan Canal. The rhythm of the avenues directed towards the Neva expanses, their expressive sculptural decor as well as the very atmosphere of the Summer Gardens retain to this day the characteristic features of Peter's "paradise". Together with the Summer Palace of Peter the Great the area stretches for some twelve hectares and served as the Tsar's summer residence

The Summer Gardens

in the period when the city was under construction. Originally the gardens were a fine example of an eighteenth-century regular *Lustgarten*, with a clear-cut layout, symmetrical avenues, fanciful cropping of trees and bushes as well as with entertaining park structures – pavilions, galleries, trellises, fountains and "a labyrinth of Aesop's fables". The garden with fine marble statues turned into a sort of "Academy", where St Petersburgers received the fundamentals of European education. The Summer Gardens have lived through several catastrophic floods and partly lost their original glitter, but became with the time a favourite place for people's promenades and rest.

THE SUMMER GARDENS
SCULPTURAL GROUP: *PEACE AND ABUNDANCE*. 1722
SCULPTOR: PIETRO BARATTA

THE SUMMER PALACE OF PETER THE GREAT. 1710–14. ARCHITECTS: DOMENICO TREZZINI, ANDREAS SCHLÜTER, NICCOLO MICHETTI, MIKHAIL ZEMTSOV. TODAY THE FORMER SUMMER RESIDENCE OF PETER THE GREAT FUNCTIONS AS A MEMORIAL MUSEUM OF HISTORY AND DAILY LIFE

THE NEVA RAILING OF THE SUMMER GARDENS. 1771–84. ARCHITECTS: YURI VELTEN, PIOTR YEGOROV

The Field of Mars

In the first quarter of the eighteenth century there was the so-called Empty Meadow between the Summer Gardens and urban quarters. Then its area was levelled, grass was sown, alleys were laid out and it turned into a place of promenades, firework displays and military parades. In the reign of Elizabeth the area received the name of Summer Meadow as there was the Tsarina's Palace of Empress Elizabeth, the "Golden Chambers", nearby. Under Paul I the meadow was renamed in the western fashion, the Field of Mars, in honour of the Roman god of war, and the area was used for military exercises, parades and reviews. Later, for nearly two centuries, the Field of Mars was a waste land, a "St Petersburg Sahara", over which clouds of sand and dust were swirling in summer, until the early twentieth century when a garden with flowerbeds and wide paths was laid out there. In 1917 the Field of Mars was used as a burial place for the victims of the February Revolution and later many participants of the October Revolution and the Civil War were interred here, too. A granite monument, *To the Fighters of the Revolution*, was installed and an "Eternal Fire" was lit up in their memory. In 1801 a monument to the great Russian soldier, Alexander Suvorov, whose heroic image is allegorically represented as Mars, was unveiled near the Field of Mars. The altar depicted next to the army leader serves to remind one about Suvorov's Italian campaign during the Napoleonic Wars; depicted lying nearby is the Pope's tiara, as well as Neapolitan and Sardinian crowns.

◀ **MONUMENT TO ALEXANDER SUVOROV. 1801**
SCULPTORS: MIKHAIL KOZLOVSKY,
FIODOR GORDEYEV; ARCHITECTS
ANDREI VORONIKHIN, ALEXANDER MIKHAILOV

The Mikhailovsky Castle

THE MIKHAILOVSKY (ENGINEERS') CASTLE. VIEW FROM THE FONTANKA RIVER
THE FAÇADE IS COMPLETED BY A SEMICIRCULAR PROJECTION WITH A FLAGSTAFF TOWER, OVER WHICH THE STANDARD OF THE EMPEROR USED TO BE HOISTED

The Mikhailovsky Castle or Palace, the most romantic building in St Petersburg, is enveloped in mysteries. It was built for himself by Paul I, one of the most tragic figures in the line of the Russian autocrats on the throne. "I want to die at the place where I was born," he is said to declare, because the castle was erected at the site of the Summer Palace of Empress Elizabeth, where he had been born. This immense structure is sometimes called Paul's dream implemented in stone. The romantic Emperor was infatuated with the medieval ideals of knighthood, but at the same time he admired the French court. The castle bears the name of Archangel Michael, the head of the heavenly host, and its construction began on his name-day. The design of the castle is sometimes attributed to Vincenzo Brenna and sometime to Vasily Bazhenov or even to Paul I himself. The Emperor, trying to erase the memory of the Catherine age, took the bulk of materials for the future castle from the demolished palace of Catherine the Great at Pelle. The marble from the uncompleted St Isaac's and parquet from the Tauride Palace were also employed. Sensing a permanent state of disquiet, Paul hastened builders and, as it would turn out, brought nearer his tragic demise. The Emperor had lived only forty days in his favourite palace before he was killed by conspirators during the night of 12 March 1801. In the 1820s the building housed the Nicholas Engineering Academy and the castle came to be known as the Engineers' Castle. Today it is a branch of the Russian Museum.

◀ THE MIKHAILOVSKY (ENGINEERS') CASTLE. 1797–1800
ARCHITECTS: VASILY BAZHENOV, VINCENZO BRENNA. 1823–24. ARCHITECT: CARLO ROSSI. THE MAIN SOUTH FAÇADE OF THE CASTLE

THE PANTELEIMON (PESTEL) BRIDGE. 1907–14
ARCHITECTS: LEV ILYIN, ALEXEI ZAZERSKY; ENGINEER: ANDJEI PSHCHENITSKI

When one walks along St Petersburg streets, building seem to step aside from time to time affording fine vistas replacing one another — now they attract one's attention by a white-columned portico or an elegant arch, now by a picturesque bend of the river and a bridge spanning it. The elegant arched Panteleimon (Pestel) Bridge across the Fontanka, the banks of which are clad in granite, cannot fail to attract one's attention. It was built on the site of the demolished suspension chain bridge erected back in the 1820s. The bridge is decorated with lamps hanging, as it were, from arrows. They recall about the military glory of St Petersburg – their stands are made in the form of a fascia of spears fixed on which are short Roman swords.

The Fontanka entered the precincts of the city only in the second half of the eighteenth century and on its banks there soon grew estates, palaces and mansions, many of which have luckily survived to this day.

THE PANTELEIMON (PESTEL) BRIDGE. DETAIL

BOATS NEAR THE BELINSKY BRIDGE SPANNING THE FONTANKA

THE TRINITY BRIDGE. 1897–1903. ARCHITECTS: V. CHABROL, R. PATOUILLARD
THIS BRIDGE, BUILT BY THE BATIGNOLLES COMPANY, FRANCE, WAS OPENED IN 1903, DURING THE CELEBRATION OF THE BICENTENARY OF ST PETERSBURG.
UNTIL 1917 IT HAD BEEN THE LONGEST IN THE CITY. THE PULKOVO MERIDIAN PASSES ACROSS THE AXIS OF THE BRIDGE

VIEW OF THE ADMIRALTY EMBANKMENT. BUILT IN 1873–74. ENGINEERS: VLADISLAV KARLOVICH, SEMION SELYANINOV
THE EMBANKMENT STRETCHES FROM DECEMBRISTS' SQUARE TO THE PALACE BRIDGE. IT OWES ITS NAME TO THE ADMIRALTY
THAT CEASED TO FUNCTION AS A SHIPBUILDING ENTERPRISE IN THIS PERIOD

VIEW OF THE PALACE BRIDGE AND THE KUSTKAMMER FROM THE ROOF OF THE WINTER PALACE. 1912–16
ENGINEER: ANDJEI PSHCHENITSKI; ARCHITECT: ROMAN MELTZER. 1977 (RECONSTRUCTION).
THE CAST-IRON RAILING OF THE BRIDGE WAS INSTALLED IN 1939. ARCHITECT: LEV NOSKOV; SCULPTOR I. KRESTOVSKY

The Large Okhta Bridge

THE LARGE OKHTA BRIDGE (PETER THE GREAT BRIDGE). 1909–11. ENGINEER: GRIGORY KRIVOSHEIN, ARCHITECT: VLADIMIR APYSHKOV

The Large Okhta Bridge (or the Peter the Great Bridge) crosses the Neva a little upstream from the spot where the Okhta River flows into it. The bridge was constructed in the early twentieth century on the then outskirts of St Petersburg and therefore builders focused their attention on a rational design and other purely practical considerations rather than architectural experiments. And although next to the bridge soars a masterpiece of the Russian Baroque — the Smolny Convent, the artistic image of the bridge does not harmonize with it at all. The ceremony of its foundation took place on 27 June 1909, the 200th Anniversary of the Battle of Poltava that glorified the Russian army. The construction was entrusted to the winners of an international competition for bridge builders that was held at the very beginning of the twentieth century under the motto «Freedom to navigation.» Sixteen projects were submitted, including eight from foreign countries, but preference was given to the hors concurs project of the Russian engineer Grigory Krivoshein and the architect Vladimir Apyshkov. This comfortable riveted bridge impresses us by its huge forms and austere granite towers-lighthouses soaring over the span that could be raised manually, too. It is very comfortable for the passage of ships, but its huge mass is too overwhelming. The bridge, however, is especially fascinating by night, when it is decorated with necklaces of lamps reflected in the water.

PETER THE GREAT WAS FULLY AWARE OF THE SIGNIFICANCE OF THE FLEET FOR THE MIGHT OF THE RUSSIAN STATE AND THEREFORE HE NOT ONLY FOUNDED HIS CAPITAL ON THE SEA SHORE, BUT MADE IT A SHIPBUILDING CENTRE. THE RUSSIAN NAVY, THAT CELEBRATED ITS TERCENTENARY IN 1996, PASSED THE WAY FROM THE BOAT OF PETER THE GREAT, THE "GRANDFATHER OF THE RUSSIAN FLEET", TO POWERFUL AIRCRAFT CARRIERS AND ROCKET CRUISERS. THROUGHOUT ITS HISTORY THE RUSSIAN SAILORS HAVE NEVER LOWERED THE ST ANDREW'S FLAG BEFORE THE ENEMY, DEFENDING THE HONOUR OF THE FATHERLAND AND THEIR SHIPS. THEIR MOTTO WAS: "DEATH IS BETTER THAN SHAME!" IN HONOUR OF THEIR DEEDS MANY OBELISKS, MONUMENTS AND CHURCHES HAVE BEEN PUT UP IN ST PETERSBURG. THE WEATHERVANE IN THE FORM OF SHIP CROWNING THE SPIRE OF THE ADMIRALTY BECAME A SYMBOL OF THE NORTHERN CAPITAL

LARGE SHIPS AT THE LIEUTENANT SCHMIDT EMBANKMENT
EVERY YEAR SHOWS A CONSIDERABLE INCREASE IN THE NUMBER OF PASSENGERS ARRIVING IN THE PORT OF ST PETERSBURG ON CRUISE VESSELS. THE PASSENGER NAVIGATION IN THE PORT BEGINS IN MAY AD ENDS IN AUTUMN

View of the Spit of Vasilyevsky Island from the Palace Embankment
The magic White Nights , when "the darkness driving from off the heavens, twilight hastes
to welcome twilight", lend the city an inimitable, unparalleled romantic atmosphere

The Mariinsky Theatre. 1847–59. Architect: Albert Cavos; 1883–86. Architect: Victor Schröter. Playing a major role in the city's artistic life, the theatre is famous for its amazingly beautiful and gifted singers, dancers and composers

The Mariinsky Theatre

THE MARIINSKY THEATRE. SCENE FROM THE OPERA *PRINCE IGOR*

The earliest theatre of St Petersburg was organized soon after the foundation of "Northern Palmyra", in 1714, at the court of Natalia Alexeyevna, the sister of Peter the Great. Active theatrical life has never abated in the city since that period and the St Petersburg ballet has established for itself one of the leading positions in world art. Among some fifty theatres now functioning in the city, the Mariinsky Opera and Ballet is hardly not the most famous stage. Named in honour of Maria Alexandrovna, the wife of Alexander II, the Mariinsky opened on Theatre Square in St Petersburg on 2 October 1860 with Mikhail Glinka's opera *Life for the Tsar*. In 1885 all performances from the neighbouring Bolshoi Theatre, the conversion of which into a Conservatoire had just started, were also transferred to the new building. The Mariinsky stage proved to be brilliantly successful for the Russian ballet and opera. Its ballet company was headed for several years by the famous Marius Petipa and among its dancers were such stars as Anna Pavlova and Waclaw Nijinsky. The country's best voices, such as the basso of Fiodor Chaliapin and the tenor of Leonid Sobinov, could be heard here. The theatre changed its title several times, but today it has regained its original name and continues to enjoy world-wide renown.

◀ **THE MARIINSKY THEATRE. THE AUDITORIUM.** THE RICH DECOR OF THE AUDITORIUM DESIGNED BY ALBERT CAVOS AND THE CEILING PAINTING EXECUTED BY THE ARTIST E. FRANCIOLLI HAVE BEEN PRESERVED IN A PERFECT STATE

The Yusupov Palace

On the bank of the Moika River, next to Theatre Square, there stretches a vast two-storeyed mansion in the austere Classical style with wings, pavilions and a majestic railing separating the courtyard from the garden. Before the Bolshevik Revolution this palace was owned by the princes of the ancient Yusupov family, one of the richest in Russia. They did not spare money acquiring superb paintings, pieces of sculpture or items of furniture and invited the best craftsmen for the decoration of the exquisite drawing rooms, studies and bedrooms. The last owner of the palace was Prince Felix Yusupov, who organized a conspiracy of monarchists against the imperial family's favourite, the mystic Grigory Rasputin, who exerted a great influence on the last Empress, Alexandra Fiodorovna. It was in this palace that during the night of 17 December 1916 the prince and his accomplices killed Rasputin treating him to poisoned cakes and threw his body into the Moika.

The Yusupov Palace. The Moorish Drawing Room. 1760s. Architect: Hippolyto Monighetti. 1890s. Architect: Alexander Stepanov
This exotic and exquisite drawing room is a tribute to the vogue of the second half of the nineteenth century when
the northern capital was infatuated with structures and interiors in the "Moorish" and "Turkish" styles

◀ **The Yusupov Palace. Private apartments of Felix Yusupov the Younger**
Present-day exhibition. By A. Beloborodov

The Naval Cathedral of St Nicholas

THE NAVAL CATHEDRAL OF ST NICHOLAS AND THE EPIPHANY. 1753–62. ARCHITECT: SAVVA CHEVAKINSKY
IN THE GARDEN NEAR THE CATHEDRAL IS INSTALLED AN OBELISK IN HONOUR OF THE HEROIC SAILORS WHO DIED IN THE BATTLE OF TSUSHIMA IN 1905

The white-blue two-storeyed Cathedral of St Nicholas, a unique example of the Elizabethan Baroque, glistening with its five gilded domes, was consecrated to St Nicholas the Miracle-Worker, the patron saint of sailors. Its slender, four-tiered bell-tower with a gilded spire, remarkable for its beautiful outlines, has always attracted artists. The rejoicing, festive image of the cathedral, one of the most revered in St Petersburg, creates a special atmosphere for the entire architectural complex. The "history and honour of Russia" live on under its vaults and the memory of the glorious deeds of the Russian Navy has been retained. Not a single generation of Russian sailors hold sacred this cathedral where prayer services and public worships have been always held.

THE NAVAL CATHEDRAL OF ST NICHOLAS AND THE EPIPHANY. INTERIOR. THE CATHEDRAL HAS RETAINED ▶
THE UNIQUE INNER DECOR OF THE BAROQUE STYLE AS IT ESCAPED LOOTING DURING THE YEARS OF SOVIET POWER

VIEW OF THE PALACE BRIDGE; THE MAIN BUILDING OF THE ADMIRALTY AND ST ISAAC'S CATHEDRAL IN AN EVENING ELECTRIC LIGHT ▶

P eterhof, originally known also as the Popov farmstead and from 1944 as Petrodvorets (Peter's Palace), is reminiscent of a sparkling diamond of unique beauty. Everything here produces an impression of a large-scale fairy-land, born, as it were, by magic from the sea that Peter the Great loved so much. The iridescent, varicoloured rainbow of the fountains' water jets seems to envelop the palaces and pavilions, parks and gardens", sculptures and decorative objects of breath-taking beauty. This seaside "paradise", the capital of fountains, an entertainment previously unknown in Russia, was opened on 15 August 1723 and had been conceived by Peter the Great as early as 1705. The imperial residence on the shore of the Gulf of Finland became a triumphal memorial symbolizing Russia's access to the Baltic sea expanses. The Great Cascade, cut into the thick of the natural shore terrace, became a sort of pedestal for the Great Palace, the focal centre of the entire Peterhof complex.

THE GREAT CASCADE. THE WEST WATERFALL STAIRCASE. *THE BORGHESE WARRIOR*. 1800 ▶
FOUNDERS EDMONDE GASTECLOUX, VASILY YEKIMOV. COPY FROM THE ORIGINAL OF THE 1ST CENTURY B.C. BY AGASIAS OF EPHESUS

THE GREAT CASCADE. THE WEST WATERFALL STAIRCASE
ACTEON (IN THE CENTRE). 1801. AFTER A MODEL BY IVAN MARTOS. *DISCOBOLUS* (RIGHT). 1800. COPY FROM THE ANCIENT ORIGINAL OF THE 5TH CENTURY B.C. BY ALCMENES. *CAPITOLINE MERCURY* (ABOVE *DISCOBOLUS*). COPY FROM AN ANCIENT ORIGINAL

THE GREAT CASCADE.
THE LOWER GROTTO. THE SIDE HALL. MASCARON
ON A KEYSTONE OVER THE ARCH OF THE LOWER GROTTO. 1723

THE GREAT CASCADE. THE EAST WATERFALL STAIRCASE
PERSEUS. **1801.** AFTER A MODEL BY FEODOSY SHCHEDRIN

VIEW OF THE POOL OF THE GREAT CASCADE AND THE ALLEY ▶▶
OF FOUNTAINS. **1715–24.** ARCHITECTS: JOHANN FRIEDRICH BRAUNSTEIN,
JEAN-BAPTISTE LE BLOND, NICCOLO MICHETTI; ENGINEER:
VASILY TUVOLKOV. **1859–60.** ARCHITECT: NIKOLAI BENOIS

VIEW OF THE GREAT PALACE THE GREAT CASCADE. 1715–24
ARCHITECTS: JOHANN FRIEDRICH BRAUNSTEIN, JEAN-BAPTISTE LE BLOND, NICCOLO MICHETTI; ENGINEER: VASILY TUVOLKOV;
FOUNTAIN MASTER: PIOTR SUALEM.1799–1806. SCULPTORS: IVAN MARTOS, IVAN PROKOFYEV, MIKHAIL KOZLOVSKY AND OTHERS

The Great Cascade, the Great Stone Grotto, three waterfall stairways and fountains with a violently rejoicing water, gilded statues of ancient gods and heroes
– all merges into a festive carnival, arrested for centuries, with all its characters of
myths and legends in some way connected with water. Leading to the central pool
is the Sea Canal, straight as an arrow. In the centre of the pool stands the figure
of Samson rending the lion's jaws from which bursts out a powerful jet of water,
twenty metres high. The memorial fountain *Samson Rending Open the Jaws of the
Lion* was erected in honour of the victory in the Battle of Poltava that decided the
outcome of the Northern War. Along the Sea Canal in the Lower Park there passes
the main axis of symmetry that underlies the scheme of entire Peterhof. The device
of «long axis» was borrowed from the vocabulary of French Classicism and implemented at Versailles, the famous luxury of which, as is supposed, Peter the Great
imitated. On the sides of the pool are situated the Italian bowl fountains and the
colonnades erected by the architect Andrei Voronikhin in 1803.

THE GREAT CASCADE.THE FOUNTAIN GROUP *SAMSON RENDING OPEN THE JAWS OF THE LION*. 1735 ▶
SCULPTOR: BARTOLOMEO CARLO RASTRELLI.1801. SCULPTOR: MIKHAIL KOZLOVSKY (CASTING).
1947. ARCHITECTS: V. SIMONOV, N. MIKHAILOV (RE-CREATION)

THE GREAT PETERHOF PALACE. THE THRONE ROOM. 1750S
ARCHITECT: BARTOLOMEO FRANCESCO RASTRELLI. 1770–78. ARCHITECT: YURI VELTEN

The Great Peterhof Palace seems to have arisen from the sea to the accompaniment of fountain jets. Its walls, green and white as the colour of sea waves, glisten in the son with the gilding of its carved decor. The palace was designed in the fanciful style of the Baroque that perfectly suited the capricious nature of Empress Elizabeth, in whose reign the residence acquired its present-day grandeur. Peter the Great, under whom the palace was known as the Hill or Upper Chamber, died before the completion of the conceived work. Thanks to the genius of Bartolomeo Francesco Rastrelli the palace gained that inimitably brilliant appearance of the imperial residence befitting the monarchs of the powerful state. The palace, stretching for nearly 300 metres and blending with the natural environment, is a superb example of the harmony of earthly and heavenly features. All subsequent alterations did not distort its integrity and it is perceived today as a stylistically integrated architectural ensemble of the eighteenth century. The decor of all the rooms in the palace, executed by Rastrelli, corresponded to the complex ceremonies of court etiquette with a deliberately pompous theatricality of life in the palace.

THE GREAT PETERHOF PALACE. THE MAIN STAIRCASE. SCULPTURE: *AUTUMN*

◀ THE GREAT PETERHOF PALACE. THE MAIN STAIRCASE.
THE UPPER LANDING. 1750S. ARCHITECT: BARTOLOMEO FRANCESCO RASTRELLI

THE MONPLAISIR PALACE. SOUTH FAÇADE. 1714–23. ARCHITECTS: JOHANN FRIEDRICH BRAUNSTEIN, JEAN-BAPTISTE LE BLOND, NICCOLO MICHETTI

Peter the Great's favourite place at Peterhof was the Palace of Monplaisir («my pleasure»), the name of which was traditional for suburban structures intended for private purposes. The palace was a typical example of the use of a «fleet teaching», one of its devices being to put up palaces as close to the water as possible and then to include festive water displays into the ensembles. The palace gave its name to the entire ensemble in the east section of the Lower Park that included, besides the Monplaisir Palace, a labyrinth and three flowerbeds with trick fountains. Each of the gardens is a small masterpiece of the art of landscape gardening and a fairly independent ensemble with the architectural structures, sculpture and fountains of its own. The palace, modest and elegant at the same time, stands right on the seashore. The glazed galleries lend it a weightless translucence and lightness and its inner layout is simple yet elegant. Peter was fond of arranging formal receptions and used to have a rest here, watching ships passing by in the Gulf of Finland. Although the palace was reconstructed and redesigned several times, many of its objects bear an imprint of Peter's age. The Hall with its unique examples of early eighteenth-century Dutch and German pieces of furniture authentically recreates the atmosphere of the past. The eight pictures by Dutch and Flemish artists adorning the walls had once formed the first collection of painting in Russia.

THE MONPLAISIR PALACE. THE HALL

THE MONPLAISIR GARDEN. CLOCHE FOUNTAIN. 1817.
AFTER A MODEL BY IVAN MARTOS

THE MONPLAISIR PALACE. THE WEST GALLERY

PETERHOF. THE CHURCH BLOCK. 1750s. ARCHITECT: BARTOLOMEO FRANCESCO RASTRELLI

Churches add much to the picturesque appearance of the south shore of the Neva bay built over with palaces and pavilions. Designed in a variety of styles, they are important attributes of the urban landscape at Peterhof, in St Petersburg and other cities of Russia. An original examples of the Neo-Russian style became the court Cathedral of SS Apostles Peter ad Paul built at Peterhof in 1895–1905 and reproducing the shapes of the sixteenth and seventeenth centuries. Contemporaries regarded it as a perfect piece of architecture. The pyramidal silhouette of the ornate cathedral is formed by five tent-shaped towers with lucarnes, turrets and stylized *kokoshnik* decorations. The unique character of the church is a rare tent-shaped design with five tops and the covered gallery for religious processions around the building. The unusual outside appearance corresponded to the church's interior decor: its iconostasis was made of majolica in imitation of its famous counterpart in the Church of St George in Venice.

PETERHOF. CATHEDRAL OF SS APOSTLES PETER AND PAUL. 1895–1905.
ARCHITECT: NIKOLAI SULTANOV

Tsarskoye Selo

The Tsarskoye Selo Palace with its sparkling golden magnificence appears before one's eyes as a fairy-tale chamber or a magic dream. This masterpiece of Baroque architecture with its exquisite luxury of fanciful forms, created by the Italian Bartolomeo Francesco Rastrelli amidst Russian fields and forests, brings to one's mind a gem of rare beauty set in an elegant mount. It is difficult to believe that once there had been the ungainly Saarskaya farmstead on this site presented by Peter to his consort Catherine and later inherited by their daughter Elizabeth. On coming to the throne, Elizabeth transformed her family's manorhouse into one of the most graceful palaces of Russia. The brilliant imperial residence grew even more majestic under its next owner, Catherine the Great.

VIGILIUS ERICKSEN
PORTRAIT OF EMPRESS ELIZABETH PETROVNA. **1758**

THE CATHERINE PALACE. ▶
DOMES OF THE CHURCH OF THE ASCENSION. 1745–56
ARCHITECTS: SAVVA CHEVAKINSKY, BARTOLOMEO FRANCESCO RASTRELLI

THE CATHERINE PALACE AND THE REGULAR PARK. 1741–56. ARCHITECTS: ANDREI KVASOV, SAVVA CHEVAKINSKY, BARTOLOMEO FRANCESCO RASTRELLI

THE CATHERINE PALACE. THE PICTURE HALL. 1750S. ARCHITECT: BARTOLOMEO FRANCESCO RASTRELLI

The Catherine Palace at Tsarskoye Selo, with its luxurious façade stretching for more than 300 metres, was the largest edifice in the period dominated by the Russian Baroque. Its inside decor – gilded mouldings, marble columns, Saxonian porcelain, velvet and damask – produces no less overwhelming impression than its glistening golden façades. The Main Staircase and the luxurious private apartments of the palace were embellished with golden carving, mirrors and amber. The grand enfilade of state rooms receded into a shining distance and an immense number of vases, columns and pieces of sculpture lend the palace an extremely majestic air. The pride of Rastrelli was the Great Hall and, as it was then called, the Large Gallery, the grandest in area of all created interiors, 850 square metres, a miracle of the great architect's mastery and precise calculation. But especially amazing was a number of two-tiered windows, a very expensive embellishment unusual for Russia, too – one should never forget about saving warmth in the cold climate. Breaking with the Russian custom, Rastrelli designed huge windows with mirrors in gilded frames on the piers. Candles lit in front of them and repeatedly reflected in the mirrors, created an illusion of an endless glistening space. Foreign guests were lost in admiration at the sight of this shining magnificence.

THE CATHERINE PALACE. SUITE OF STATE ROOMS («THE GOLDEN ENFILADE») ▶
VIEW FROM THE CRIMSON PILASTER ROOM. 1750S. ARCHITECT: BARTOLOMEO FRANCESCO RASTRELLI

The Catherine Palace. The Amber Room. 1755
ARCHITECT: BARTOLOMEO FRANCESCO RASTRELLI

THE CATHERINE PALACE. THE AMBER ROOM. 1750s
DETAIL OF THE PANEL WITH AN AMBER FRAME AND THE FLORENTINE MOSAIC *SENSE AND SMELL*

The unique Amber Room, the walls of which were adorned with panels of various kinds of amber, struck guests most. Academician Alexander. Fersman, a connoisseur of gems and semiprecious stones, called this room the «eighth miracle of the world». The unrivalled miracle was produced in Prussia, the main centre of the production of art works in amber, the fashion for which spread over Europe in the middle of the eighteenth century. The idea to create a room of «sun stone» appeared in the palace of the Prussian kings and the architect Andreas Schlüter created its project. The panels were produced by a group of amber craftsmen led by Gottfried Turau and Gottfried Tissaud. Having invited Schlüter to the Russian service, Peter the Great, who was not indifferent to all kinds of rarities, learned from the architect about this room and soon received it as a diplomatic gift from King Frederick William I. But Peter himself lived not enough to enjoy the amber panels: they were not demonstrated until 1743 when the craftsman A. Martelli arranged the Amber Room in the Winter Palace. However, the panels did not hung for a long time there, because by orders of Empress Elizabeth the precious pieces were carefully brought in hands to Tsarskoye Selo, where Bartolomeo Francesco Rastrelli designed the Amber Room for them. In the places where amber was not sufficient, he added Florentine mosaics of varicoloured jasper in amber frames. It was in this room that the rulers of Russia, beginning with Elizabeth, gave audiences for foreign ambassadors and naturally astounded them. In 1941 the Nazis occupied Tsarskoye Selo and ravaged the Amber Room. The traces of the masterpiece have been lost and searches for them continue to this day. Nevertheless the Amber Room has now been completely recreated to its former brilliance.

THE CATHERINE PALACE. THE AMBER ROOM. DETAIL OF THE LARGE FRAME ON THE SOUTH WALL

THE UPPER TIER OF THE AMBER ROOM DECOR. DETAIL

THE CATHERINE PALACE. THE AMBER ROOM. PARIS CHANDELIER-CLOCK IN THE FORM OF TREE WITH A PASTORAL SCENE. *CA 1750*

THE AMBER ROOM. FLORENTINE MOSAIC: *EYE-SIGHT*. **1750s**
RE-CREATED IN 1997 BY THE STONE-CUTTERS AND RESTORERS B. IGDALOV, R. SHAFEYEV, B. MINTS AND OTHERS

THE CATHERINE PARK. THE TURKISH BATH PAVILION. 1829
ARCHITECT: HIPPOLYTO MONIGHETTI

THE CATHERINE PARK. FOUNTAIN: *GIRL WITH A PITCHER.* **1810–17.**
SCULPTOR: PAVEL SOKOLOV. 1996. BRONZE. COPY FROM THE ORIGINAL
BY PAVEL SOKOLOV. ENGINEER: AUGUSTIN DE BÉTHENCOURT

THE CATHERINE PARK. THE MARBLE (SIBERIAN OR PALLADIAN) BRIDGE. 1770–76. ARCHITECT: VASILY NEYELOV

◄ THE CATHERINE PARK. THE CAMERON GALLERY. 1782–86. ARCHITECT: CHARLES CAMERON

MONUMENT TO ALEXANDER PUSHKIN IN THE LYCEUM GARDEN. 1900. SCULPTOR: ROBERT BACH

Pavlovsk

PAVLOVSK. THE GREAT PALACE. THE GREEK HALL. 1789. ARCHITECTS: CHARLES CAMERON, VINCENZO BRENNA. 1803–04. ARCHITECT: ANDREI VORONIKHIN

P avlovsk occupies a special place among the palace and park imperial complexes. Created later than others, it is full of charm and subtle taste and has few equals in elegance. Nature and art are combined here in an inimitable and graceful harmony and dispose one to solitude, meditation and dreams. The year of the foundation of Pavlovsk is 1777, when Empress Catherine the Great presented the village of Pavlovskoye to her son, Tsesarevich Pavel Petrovich, and his consort on the occasion of the birth of their first child, the future Emperor Alexander I. The Tsesarevich put the presented estate at the full disposal of his consort, Princess Sophie Dorothea of Württemberg, Maria Fiodorovna after accepting the Orthodox faith. Pavlovsk turned out to be closely associated with her memory as the mother of Emperors Alexander I and Nicholas I. The harmonious ensemble with the palace, park and various structures in the park was created at Pavlovsk by the Scottish architect Charles Cameron, who brought the Neo-Greek style to St Petersburg. The elegant silhouette of the Palladian-style palace, reminding us of Italian villas, stands at the top of a gently sloping hill reflecting in the waters of the Slavianka River.

◀ **PAVLOVSK. VIEW OF THE GREAT PALACE AND THE CENTAUR BRIDGE. 1782–86**
ARCHITECT: CHARLES CAMERON; 1796–99. ARCHITECT: VINCENZO BRENNA
BRIDGE. 1799. ARCHITECT: CHARLES CAMERON

Contents